PREVIOUS OFFENCES

Sussex crimes and punishments in the past

GW00545670

W H Johnson

S.B. Publications

By the same author
Early Victorian Alfriston
Crime and Disorder in Late Georgian Alfriston
Brighton's First Trunk Murderer
The Macaroni Dancers and other stories

First published in 1997 by S. B. Publications,
c/o 19 Grove Road, Seaford, East Sussex BN25 1TP

ISBN 1 85770 123 2

Designed and typeset by CGB, Lewes
Printed by Island Press Ltd.
3 Cradle Hill Industrial Estate, Seaford, East Sussex BN25 3JE
Telephone: (01323) 490222

CONTENTS

	Page
Introduction	4
1 The Novice Highwaymen	7
Gleanings 1800–1801	13
2 The Ten Shilling Man	15
Gleanings 1802–1805	21
3 A Maresfield Mystery	23
Gleanings 1807–1810	30
4 Three and a Half Dozen Pigeons	31
Gleanings 1811–1813	36
5 The Shipley Gang	37
Gleanings 1815–1817	40
6 Arson at Alfriston	43
Gleanings 1819–1832	49
7 Hard Times	52
Gleanings 1835–1838	57
8 A Caste Apart	61
Gleanings 1839–1850	71
9 Passion and Poison	76
Gleanings 1851	84
Bibliography	88

ABOUT THE AUTHOR

W H 'Johnnie' Johnson, winner of the South East Arts Prose Prize in 1991, first came to Sussex in 1956 and has lived here, off and on, ever since. For many years he was a Comprehensive School Head and later a Schools Inspector. Writing is now his principal interest. He also lectures on local history and the origin of surnames and gives prose and poetry readings. He tends to specialise in the history of crime because, he says, 'it is such an important social and economic factor and also because its narrative, its drama, enthralls me.'

INTRODUCTION

ONE ought perhaps to have some purpose for bringing together such a concourse of people, wicked and innocent, cunning and gullible, the dull and the hopeless, the weak, the bullying, the feckless, the irredeemably stupid and the positively dangerous.

Here they are, all lined up on one side or other of the law, with as much of their stories as historical documentation permits. But the purpose? Perhaps it is simply to offer proof that if ever there was a Golden Age, a crime–free era, it was certainly not in those twenty or thirty years on each side of Victoria's accession.

I am intrigued, not surprised, to find so many resonances of the present here – the bawling harridan threatening her husband; the violent robbers who leave householders still fearful, months after their visits; young boys, impervious to punishment and advice alike, immersed so deep in crime, yet with whom the courts can do nothing; the wife whose passion leads her on to murder; the stealers of horses (rather than cars); the 'blacklegs', present at every race track, fleecing unwary 'pigeons' with their rigged gambling devices.

Each of the nine crimes recounted here is different in kind and each one is followed by extracts, principally from newspapers, of other criminal activities which may deepen the reader's understanding of both the topic and the period.

A word about the period. In the first half of the nineteenth century there were vast changes in town and country, brought about by technological and commercial revolutions. These were responsible not just for the nation's economic advancement but also for great distress among the already poorest classes. There were more people than jobs, especially in agriculture. The vast ranks of the impoverished were relieved by meagre, frequently grudging, hand–outs from the parish. Poverty and crime went hand in hand, just as much in the countryside as in the haphazard slums of Brighton and other towns. That is not to say, of course, that all crimes were committed by the poor.

It is not possible to estimate how much crime there was during the first half of the nineteenth century. Certainly there was public concern over what was regarded as its constant increase, although there is no way of assessing how great that increase might have been.

Until 1840 most policing in the county was the responsibility of unpaid parish constables, elected by the local vestries. In some places, in response to public alarm, patrols were introduced on occasion. Naturally none of these part time, amateur arrangements could restrain really determined offenders.

In two of the cases covered, professional officers from London were sent for as the parish constables – mostly local tradesmen – had not the required skills to solve crimes. Later in the period, however, as the inquiries into the activities of the Isaacs Gang (A Caste Apart) demonstrate, a more successful investigative touch was evident in the county police forces.

The system of law and sentencing at the beginning of the century permitted capital punishment for more than two hundred offences. This so-called Bloody Code proved increasingly unworkable. Many judges and juries found it brutal and offensive and often, in consequence, the manifestly guilty were acquitted or at least, had their charges reduced. At other times, when there was no alternative to the cruel rigidities of the system, judges, sometimes tearful, passed death sentences they knew to be unjust. But this was changing. By 1830, the Code would be softened, at least by the standards of the times.

There was transportation, of course, and while it was effective in a certain sense – it took the troublemakers out of circulation without the costly recourse to imprisonment – some welcomed it. In fact, in 1830 a pamphlet extolling the virtues of Australia was circulated in Lewes gaol.

However, after a peak from 1831 to 1840 when 51,200 people were 'boated', numbers declined until, in response to remonstrations from the settlers, convict transportation petered out, the last dribble being sent to Western Australia in 1868.

From then, Britain had to attempt to look after all of its lawbreakers. Had to build more prisons for them and had to try to work out what such places were for.

W H Johnson
Eastbourne
March 1997

✻

*The capture of Bob Bignall,
the Ten Shilling Man, was
the subject of this print
published in 1807.
It shows – in sections – his
capture, his attempted escape
from Lewes Gaol and his
execution at Horsham.*

✻

1

THE NOVICE HIGHWAYMEN

IT is a stiff haul, this stretch of road just beyond Forest Row. It is a long, steep, taxing drive up Wall Hill and the horse drawn post cart trundles slowly through a black, silent, midnight world. Perhaps the driver is dozing, for he has been on his journey from Brighton for the past five hours. A quarter of an hour ago, back at Forest Row, he took on some more mail bags. In another three quarters of an hour or so he will unload others at East Grinstead. In the meantime he needs just to twitch the reins gently and catnap the minutes away. There is a long night ahead of him and a long morning, too, as the post cart creeps towards Croydon and then on to London.

There is nothing new here for William Edwards or indeed for any of the postboys who cover this route six nights a week, lone travellers in a dark landscape. They are used to all weathers; used to foul, wretched runs when they have to dismount to lead the horses, hock high in mud, along the clogged highway.

But this July night is not like that. The road surface may be pock-marked and torn but it is dry and firm. Tonight Edwards can sit on the box and wait for East Grinstead. Let it come to him. He can doze his way there.

Then he hears voices.

Unexpected scuffling from the side of the road.

A man, two men.

One of them has seized the reins.

Edwards hears the threat, sees the pistol, and sensibly does as he is told.

The Great Mail Robbers of 1801 escaped with something in the region of £500,000 in today's terms. Only two men were involved and they were not practised criminals, in fact there can rarely have been a more unlikely pair of thieves. Not only were they first offenders but most astonishing of all, one of them was seventy years of age.

What was it that led to so old a man, not previously guilty of any criminal offence, to engage in a crime of such daring and one for which, if he were caught, would lead to the hangman's noose? Come to that, what drove the younger man, a twenty-seven year old shopkeeper, to commit highway robbery?

Major crimes are committed for a variety of reasons – greed, lust, revenge, need, daring – or out of sheer wickedness. In the case of John Beatson and his stepson, William, the motive must have been desperation.

Highway robbery was so alien to their characters. Given their history it would have been far less remarkable had their offence been swindling, deception or fraud. Their backgrounds were respectable. At one time John Beatson had been a sailor and when he came ashore he had opened a public house, The College Tavern, in Edinburgh. There he and his wife adopted an infant, William Whalley, and brought him up as their own child. The affection which John had for his stepson was undiminished to the end.

The public house prospered and it was eventually handed over to William. John, by then widowed, came south to London to take up a position as a butler. Some years later, when his wife died, William sold the tavern and joined his stepfather in London where he opened a wine shop in Covent Garden, later moving the business to Kennington.

There is nothing to explain the moves to London. Why should John Beatson, a Scotsman now in his sixties, elect to make such a radical change in his life and why should his stepson sell an apparently thriving public house and decide to rent a shop in a strange city?

Yet such decisions are not necessarily suspect for it seems that the roots of the Great Mail Robbery lay in circumstances which occurred after the Beatsons' arrival in London. John found himself out of work and William's business failed. More or less at the same time the two men were in severe financial difficulties. and the result of these two parallel strokes of ill luck was astonishing.

At the start they had some small savings and they did not have to face the indignity of throwing themselves on the parish. But if matters did not improve there would be no alternative. Facing them was a descent from a modest independence and security into the gnawing, shameful uncertainties of dire poverty. Once down it would be impossible, certainly in the case of the older man, to expect any restoration of their previous fortunes. The Beatsons were unwilling to accept such a fate. For them desperate circumstances demanded desperate measures.

In the early summer of 1801 the two men went to stay in the village of

Hartfield on the edge of Ashdown Forest. It seems that they knew the area and that they already had a plan. John Beatson posed as a gentleman coming into the country for health reasons and his stepson accompanied him as his servant. William made no secret of his surname but for the purpose of the charade John adopted another name.

During their stay at Hartfield they worked on the details of their plan to rob the Brighton to London mail coach. It was a prime and easy target for it was known to carry considerable sums of money and always to be driven by one man, who was not armed..

They had to decide the best time and place to effect the robbery and the best way of escape with their loot. At Hartfield, which was close to the mail coach's route, they were ideally situated to explore the area of the forest through which it would pass..

Every night, except Saturday, the mail coach left Brighton at seven o'clock. It carried mail bags from several towns in the south of the country, dropping off some at East Grinstead and others at Croydon. The remainder were destined for the capital. As there was no service on the Saturday a double load was carried on the Sunday. It was the Sunday collection that the Beatsons intended to steal.

They reasoned that the best time to stop the mail coach was about midnight for this would allow them four or five hours of darkness in which to effect their escape. They planned to strike on Wall Hill, an ideal stopping place just beyond Forest Row and two miles short of East Grinstead.

Having agreed their plan, the respectable elderly gentleman and his servant said their farewells to Hartfield, telling the people they met there that they were returning to Windsor. As it was, they went back to their home in Mount Street, London but they were soon to come back to Sussex.

On Saturday, 18 July 1801, the two unlikely robbers took the stage coach as far as Godstone where they stayed the night at the Rose and Crown. The following morning they went on to Blindley Heath, eating dinner at the Blue Anchor. At about eight o'clock that evening, a witness at their trial was to recall, they were on East Grinstead Common, nearing the meadow on Wall Hill where they would await the coming of the mail coach.

The impression the Beatsons gave, travelling as they did by coach, staying at an inn, mixing in dining rooms, was of solid, respectable dependentabilty. No one suspected that the tall elderly gentleman and his young well–mannered companion were about to pull off a major crime.

Some time after midnight on Monday, 20 July, the mail cart was stopped by two men described in the newspapers as footpads. The postboy, threatened with a pistol, had led his cart into the meadow in which the robbers had waited. Once there the horse was unhitched and the mail bags, ten of them, were taken off. Although cumbersome they were not unduly large and heavy and the two highwaymen – for that is what they now were – could manage them well enough.

Before his assailants left him they warned the postboy, Edwards, that if he stirred from the spot before the expiration of an hour, he would have his brains blown out by one of their companions who was in concealment. No doubt it was this threat that delayed his arrival in East Grinstead until about two o'clock, when he raised a hue and cry. By then there was no sign any mail bag thieves. Although search parties scoured the highway on horseback, there was no trace of the men who had carried out the Great Mail Robbery.

The Beatsons had, in fact, taken a cross country route to the east and north through fields and woods, along hedges and narrow farm tracks, over fences and stiles. They were on foot, lugging the bags, and although on their exploratory visit they must have assessed the way they were now taking, they could not have known the countryside in detail and must, in the dark, have found their passage extremely difficult.

Why had they not equipped themselves with a gig or with horses? Perhaps they knew that any pursuit would be by road in which case they might be overtaken. They were not unique in arriving at that conclusion. Many burglars and thieves preferred escape routes across meadows and heathlands, skirting towns and large villages until they were sufficiently far away from the scene of their crime. This was precisely how the Isaacs Gang operated fifty years later.

By dawn the robbers had passed Hartfield, where only weeks earlier they had prepared their strategy. Now that it was light they were able to examine carefully what it was they had stolen. Here, in a cornfield, they abandoned some of the bags in which they left nearly £10,000 in drafts and bills. But they kept £4,000 in bank notes.

In the middle of the morning they reached Westerham, fifteen miles or so from Wall Hill. They were now in some disarray and looked far less respectable than they had done on the previous day. William was limping badly and the old man was obviously very tired.

The two bedraggled strangers almost straightaway expressed an anxiety about hiring a coach to take them to Deptford, where they said they lived. They would pay anything they told Mrs Turney, the landlady of The Chequers. She was uneasy about the two men, particularly when they offered a £2 note to pay the two shilling bill for their meal. She was accustomed to all manner of men calling at her inn, many of them travel–stained. What worried her about these two strangers was the general nervousness of their manner and their anxiety to hire transport and be gone. She remembered them all right, the older man in his green coat and black waistcoat, the smaller man wearing black.

Mrs Turney was not the only person to be surprised by the men's behaviour. When they came to pay for the hire of a chaise, William brought a fistful of notes out of his pocket and this incident was to be recalled by a witness at their trial the following year.

The two Beatsons took the chaise to Deptford, accompanied by a mounted man who was to return the vehicle to Westerham. He noticed that on arrival they then transferred to a coach which was to take them on to London. Yet they had said their home was in Deptford. That seemed suspicious to him.

Now they were in the city the two robbers must have felt more secure for they could expect to blend in and be safe from detection. Nevertheless, after a week they decided to go to Liverpool, intending to go on to Ireland. They hired another chaise and taking their dog, Emma, with them they set off for the north west.

The General Post Office, only hours after the robbery, had offered a £200 reward for information leading to the capture of the robbers. In the next few days they received some leads and, while the

GENERAL POST-OFFICE,

Monday Morning, 20th July, 1801.

THE Poſt Boy conveying the Mail from Lewes to Eaſt Grinſtead, was ſtopt this Morning within about two Miles and a Quarter of Eaſt Grinſtead, by two Men on Foot, who robbed him of the following Bags of Letters, namely

Brighton,
Shoreham,
Steyning, } for London.
Lewes,
AND
Uckfield,

and Five Bye-Bags, viz. Brighton for Croydon, ditto for Eaſt Grinſtead, ditto for Lewes, Lewes for Croydon, ditto for Eaſt Grinſtead.

Whoever ſhall apprehend and convict, or cauſe to be apprehended and convicted, the Perſons who committed this Robbery, will be entitled to a Reward of TWO HUNDRED POUNDS, over and above the Reward given by Act of Parliament for apprehending Highwaymen: ſ Or if either of the Perſons concerned therein will ſurrender himſelf, and make Diſcovery, whereby the other Perſon who committed the Robbery may be apprehended and brought to Juſtice, ſuch Diſcoverer will be entitled to the ſaid Reward, and will alſo receive His Majeſty's moſt gracious Pardon.

By Command of His Majeſty's Poſtmaſter-General,

FRANCIS FREELING,
SECRETARY.

Beatsons were on their way north, some new handbills describing one of the wanted men were being sent around the country.

The *Sussex Weekly Advertiser* of 3 August told its readers: 'Yesterday morning handbills were received here from the General Post Office describing the person of William Whalley Beatson as one of the men who robbed the mail near East Grinstead on the 20th of last month. He is of genteel appearance and assumes the title of Esquire.'

Apparently nobody had, as yet, realised his stepfather's part in the affair.

On Sunday 2 August, the Beatsons spent the night at The Angel at Knutsford in Cheshire. On the following day, only a short time after they had left for Liverpool, handbills arrived at the inn from the General Post Office. Immediately the innkeeper realised who it was that he had had under his roof the previous night. He remembered the dog and its collar which bore the legend 'Wm. Beatson, Mount Street, Grosvenor Square, London' and got in touch with a surveyor employed by the Post Office, who was staying nearby.

The surveyor set off in pursuit of the robbers, followed them to Liverpool and within hours had located the inn where they had taken a room. He alerted the local constables and, with a lawyer in attendance, they burst in on the Beatsons and arrested them.

Any doubts they might have had about the guilt of their prisoners was dispelled when they opened their trunk. Here they found £1,700 in notes, a letter from the Lewes mail and a pistol. More than £1,000 was found in their pockets.

Escorted by Bow Street officers the Beatsons returned to London where they underwent examination. The magistrates at Bow Street, confident that they had the mail cart robbers before them, had them transferred to Horsham to await trial at the next Assizes.

The trial of John and William Beatson took place at Horsham in March 1802. In a noble enough attempt to assume sole responsibility for what had occurred at Wall Hill, John proposed that his stepson should turn King's Evidence and appear as chief prosecution witness.

But the prosecution had no need of William.

A further defence that John Beatson had been given the notes by a man who had returned from India and who was in his debt, was rejected.

While in gaol at Horsham, William Beatson and another prisoner attempted to escape. When the turnkey was diverted they got into the prison yard and threw strips of blanket over the wall to give the impression that they had got away. In fact, they hid in the prison sewer. After some hours, assuming that the intensity of the search would have died down, they came out of hiding. They were so cold, however, that they could not manage to climb the wall and were easily recaptured.

In the course of the two day trial, a procession of witnesses, twenty six in all – among them innkeepers, the postboy, residents of Hartfield, the Post Office surveyor, a mason from Westerham – all offered incontestable evidence of the guilt of the accused. What did impress the onlookers, however, was the demeanour of both men. Only once did they falter when the verdict was given and the sentences pronounced. It was only then that the two men fainted.

As was customary with mail robbers, they were to be executed near the scene of their crime. Can it have been any consolation to learn that the humane judge had decided that their bodies should not hang in chains as a warning to others? Their friends were to be allowed to bury them at home.

Early on Saturday, 17 April, they left Horsham gaol to make the slow, twenty mile journey to Wall Hill, where, just off the road, the gallows awaited them. There was a dense crowd of three thousand, some of them perched in trees the better to see the Beatsons hanged, side by side.

'The old man who appeared as it were to spring from the cart as it was drawn from under him, died without a struggle; but the young one exhibited strong symptoms of life for near a quarter of an hour after he was suspended, owing to the shifting of the rope, which was not skilfully placed by the executioner,' reported the *Sussex Weekly Advertiser*, adding with some satisfaction: 'Their behaviour to and at the place of execution was truly penitential and becoming men in their unhappy situations.'

But then, save for this one aberration, they seem always to have behaved well.

GLEANINGS 1800-1801

17 March 1800

Yesterday morning the High Sheriff and his attendants passed through this town, on their way to the Assizes, which commenced this day, at Horsham. The dress of the Javelin-men exhibited a novelty as pleasing to the eye as it was creditable to the taste and liberality of the Sheriff. It consists of a superfine scarlet frock, with black velvet collar, and yellow buttons, bearing the letters GR beneath the crown; waistcoat of the same colour; new buckskin breeches; and a velvet jockey-cap; the cap is, however, at Horsham to be abandoned for a very large cocked-up hat, it having been furnished merely as a convenience for travelling.

14 July 1800

A few days since, about five o'clock in the afternoon, the house of a little farmer in the parish of Chailey was, in the absence of the family, who were haymaking, entered at the backdoor by two men, it is supposed with the hope of finding money but being disappointed in their expectations, they contented themselves with carrying off a few trifling articles, the most valuable of which was a new shirt. Two men with dirty smock frocks and sticks in their hands were observed to pass the house and supposed to be the robbers.

2 March 1801

A CAUTION – A man of low stature, swarthy complexion, with hair a little grey and queued to the fashion, wearing dark-colour'd clothes and short spatterdashes bound with red, and who travels with a portfolio or parcel at his back, on his way from Battle to Horsebridge, on Thursday last, imposed on several persons by selling them watches for two guineas and a half and three guineas, though in reality not worth one guinea. He facilitates the imposition by pretending to be a Hungarian man-cook, out of place, and in great distress, which compels him to part with his watch as the only means left of procuring subsistence.

From the *Sussex Weekly Advertiser*

❑ ❑ ❑ ❑ ❑ ❑

2

THE TEN SHILLING MAN

WHATEVER else may be said about Bob Bignall, he quit this life with style. Like any other man called to Horsham Hang Fair to answer for his misdeeds, he arrived in a horse drawn cart, sitting on his coffin. But of Bignall there was an expectation – for was he not a well known criminal to whom a distinct touch of glamour was attached.

Four years earlier – in 1803 – when charged with murder he had been fortunate to escape the noose. Years before that, and indeed ever since, he had made his name as a burglar, poacher and footpad. He was already on the run from Rochester gaol when he was arrested at Ditchling. While waiting, after his capture, in Lewes House of Correction to be transferred to the more secure gaol at Horsham, he just failed to effect a spectacular escape. Now, about to be hanged when still aged only twenty–seven, Bob Bignall was something of a celebrity.

On 4 April 1807, when the cart edged slowly through the crowd of three thousand spectators from the gaol to the public gallows, the condemned man conducted himself 'with almost unexampled fortitude', betraying not the slightest fear. Nor, when the cart stopped at the scaffold which was surrounded by men of the West Essex Militia, did he appear other than calm. Indeed, he did all that the mob expected of him.

In his dark, close fitting greatcoat and his fine boots, Bignall accompanied the clergyman in prayer. Indeed, some of the prayers he had chosen for the occasion himself.

Then, standing foursquare on the flat bed of the cart, in a loud voice he made the kind of farewell speech that hanging mobs felt themselves entitled to hear. He warned his listeners against what he called 'the prevailing vices of the time'. Let them not profane the Lord's day, he warned them. Let them not indulge in idleness, whoredom, dishonesty, drunkenness. Let them not abuse the confidence of their masters. He stood before them, a prime example of what befell those whose lives were not conducted in accordance with the highest principles. He commended his family to the mercy of the world, declaring them innocent of the crimes he had committed. Then, offering his spirit to the disposal of God, he awaited his punishment.

When the hangman adjusted the halter, Bignall asked him not to bungle his task. But public executioners often brought little professional skill to their work. Seconds later, the rump of the horse was slapped and it trundled away from under the gallows, taking the cart from under the feet of the condemned man. There was no trapdoor, no sharp tug of the rope being jerked by a falling body, no broken neck, no sudden finish. Bignall was left struggling, dangling, strangling at the rope's end.

At last, when it was all over, the body was left on display long enough to satisfy the spectators – long enough for them to view it, to joke or sneer or moralise, to point out to their children what happened to those who misbehaved. A couple of women with goitre were allowed to reach up, to take the dead man's hand in theirs, to stroke their swollen necks with it. And then, when the crowds drifted away, Bignall's wife paid the hangman a guinea for her husband's clothes. She would take him home to his grave and they would go in a cart and he would be clothed.

This was an important hanging. Years after, people would date other events from Bignall's execution. 'It would be about the time Bignall was hanged,' they would say. They might not recall the year as 1807 but they would remember the occasion as a significant point in the local time scale and deeds and events would be accorded their place before or after Bignall's hanging.

Bignall first came to the attention of a wide public in March 1803 when he appeared before Mr Justice Heath at Horsham Assizes, charged with the murder of the smuggler, Jack Webber.

One of the newspaper accounts of the shooting of Webber at Stone Pound near Hassocks describes Bignall, then twenty–two, as a 'notorious character' for he had already been in trouble on several occasions. Elsewhere he is referred to as the 'noted Bob Bignall' and, in another account, he is dismissed scornfully as 'a ten–shilling man', a title given to informants assisting the Excise Service against smugglers. Perhaps it was thought ironic that a man of such dubious reputation, one who had himself most likely engaged in smuggling, should inform on others in the trade and, worse, that he should kill a smuggler.

What is certain about the events of the evening of 30 November, 1802, is that Jack Webber, a farmer's son, and half a dozen others, all on horseback, were on their way from Patcham to their homes in and around Hurstpierpoint. At Stone Pound, where they met Bignall and Joseph Howe, an Excise Officer, there were raised voices, some blows exchanged and a shot was fired. Webber was badly wounded and he and his companions rode off to seek medical help.

The following day Bignall and Howe reported what had happened to the Excise Supervisor in Lewes. Perhaps they expected to be congratulated but were instead severely reprimanded for there had been no evidence that the men they met were carrying contraband. Later in the day, after the matter had been reported to the magistrates, Howe was arrested at Rottingdean and Bignall was found hiding in a cave by the seashore. Both were taken to Lewes House of Correction to await trial.

Webber lingered for a week and after his death Bignall was charged with wilful murder and taken to Horsham to await trial. Howe was released – his claim to having been lying unconscious at the time of the shooting serving to exonerate him. However, he was straightaway dismissed from the Excise Service for other misdemeanours.

The Assize court heard how the two parties met at about 9pm on a country road. An independent witness said that he heard Bignall shout out: 'Stop or I shall shoot you.'

Webber had replied: 'What do you stop me for on the King's highway?'

As neither he nor the men with him were carrying any contraband on that occasion, Webber might well have felt at liberty to put such an indignant question.

Then came Bignall's voice again: 'Go on and I shall shoot you.' And then a shot was heard.

Webber called out that he had been hit and Bignall, brandishing another pistol, ran up to one of Webber's companions, Richard Pratt and shouted: 'Is there any more of you smuggling rascals coming? If there is I'll blow your lives out.'

At this point Webber and the others had ridden off.

Pratt's version of what happened is broadly similar. He said the party had just turned off the road and into a meadow which would lead them by the quickest way to Hurstpierpoint. He heard Bignall call out: 'Is this your nighest road home, Mr Webber – and you, Pratt – I'll mark you too.'

In the darkness Pratt had made out the figures of Bignall and Howe and the latter was carrying a pistol in one hand and a sword in the other.

'Damn your eyes' he had shouted, 'we will blow your brains out."

'We have got nothing on our horses now. You have no right to stop us,' Pratt had answered. Then came the pistol shot.

In court Bignall did not deny that he had fired his pistol but he claimed that he and Howe, faced by Webber and his friends, feared for their lives. The two of them, Bignall said, had been out looking for smugglers and had seen Webber's party at Stone Pound. Outnumbered and fearful, they had hidden behind a hedge for safety but were spotted.

Howe's testimony backed up Bignall's. He said he had heard Webber shout: 'Here's that bloody exciseman and that rogue Bignall.' Pratt had called out, as he led his horse into the meadow: 'Let's follow them and murder them.'

Howe told the court that he and Bignall ran up the field and over a fence but Webber and Pratt pursued them, leaping on horseback over the rails. They then doubled back and made a dash into the garden of a house by the roadside. Again, they were chased, their pursuers riding up to the garden railings where Webber dismounted and encouraged his followers with shouts of: 'Damn their bloody eyes. Let us murder them both.' The rest of the men beat their sticks on the railings and uttered frightening threats.

It was then, Howe said, that he realised his attempts to cool matters down had failed so he drew his sword. 'I can hold out no longer,' he had shouted.'I must defend myself.'

'Damn your eyes,' Webber had answered. 'Why don't you shoot me through the body, you damned excising bugger, for I would rather die than live.'

At this point Webber had reached over the fence and hit Howe with a large knobbed stick. The blow knocked him unconscious and he did not come round until he recognised Mary Warner, the woman of the house, dabbing his forehead with a damp cloth. The smugglers had ridden off. No, Howe told the court, he had not heard any shot fired. He had been unconscious when Bignall used his pistol.

After a trial lasting five hours, the jury found Bignall not guilty. Perhaps they felt that a man alone, as he had been, had every right to defend himself against seven others who were threatening his life. With Howe lying senseless on the ground, what else could he do?

Few can have been more fortunate than Bignall, for the jury, impressed perhaps by Howe's version of the matter, had ignored the significant testimony of the accused man's cousin.

Earlier in the evening of the shooting John Bignall had met his cousin

Bob and they had seen Webber on his horse nearby.

'Yonder goes Jack Webber highly mounted,' Bob Bignall had said, 'but I'll dismount him before morning.'

What had he meant by this? That he would catch him smuggling that night and with Howe, arrest him? Or was it a threat? Or a promise? Had Bignall already planned to confront Webber that night and, acting under the protection of the law, to shoot him? Certainly Bignall had cause to dislike the smuggler who, along with Pratt and another man, had recently attacked and beaten him at a fair, presumably because of Bignall's activities against smuggling.

The following morning, when John Bignall met his cousin again, he was told: 'I have tapped the man who I told you last night that I would if I had the opportunity before morning.' Thomas Stevens, who was present and heard the boastful remark, asked Bignall if he had shot the man or the horse. Bignall replied that he had 'shot the great Jack Webber'. He went on to say that the ball had entered somewhere about the navel. He did not believe that he was dead but thought he could not live long.

Such testimony does suggest that the murder of Jack Webber was not the result of a chance encounter but premeditated. Bignall certainly seems to have been fortunate to be acquitted.

❏ ❏ ❏ ❏ ❏

Despite his narrow escape, Bignall did not alter his ways. Over the next three or four years his life of crime continued, sometimes alone, at other times with accomplices. For a period he was employed in the Excise Service at Bristol – most likely in a similar capacity to that which he had fulfilled in Sussex. Then, for some unspecified reason, he returned to the south east.

At some stage he teamed up with John Tingley, another Sussex man, probably, like Bignall, from the Clayton area. If so, the pair of them are likely to have committed robberies and burglaries in Somerset where Tingley was eventually to hang.

It was possibly with Tingley and a third man that Bignall burgled the house of a Mr Preston at Warbleton near Heathfield in February 1806. They knocked at the door and when it was opened two of them burst into the house, threatening the occupants with their pistols. The third man stayed outside, acting as a look out.

When Preston refused to tell the intruders where his money was kept he was viciously beaten. Eventually, bleeding profusely and unable to stand more punishment, he told the thieves that his money was kept in the escritoire from which they took £70. They then dragged the frightened man down to the cellar where they drank beer, complaining that it was 'damned bad' and telling him to buy a better quality for their next visit. When they left, the men took a bottle of brandy with them.

In the following months Bignall and Tingley were involved in a succession of similar crimes until in the summer of 1806 they were arrested in Kent and lodged in Rochester gaol. On 13 September, before they came to trial, the two men escaped together.

The next month Bignall and Tingley made a daylight raid on the house of a wealthy farmer, John Wickham, at Albourne. They had kept it under observation, watching the farm workers going about their tasks. When the coast was clear they entered the house, taking Wickham by surprise. They forced him into the bedroom and bound him to the bed, taking his watch and a small amount of money including two seven shilling pieces. At this point they discovered that the housekeeper had managed to escape through a window and was raising the alarm. They fled.

This was their last crime. Wickham had recognised Bignall, who had lived in the area for much of his life. He was born at Clayton only a few miles away and at the time of this crime was living there. Soon a daylight hunt involving two hundred men was on for the two burglars who had gone to ground in the woods between Henfield and Hurstpierpoint.

In the early hours of the next morning the robbers thought it safe to move. Some time between five and six o'clock, they were walking through Ditchling when Harriott, publican of The White Horse, recognised them and bravely tackled them. Tingley managed to struggle free but his partner could not get away, nor did Tingley stay to help him. Bignall was overpowered and finally, with the help of others alerted by the uproar, he was arrested and taken to Lewes House of Correction.

Bignall's ingenuity did not fail him even then. While waiting in the prison yard for the postchaise summoned to take him to Horsham, he found a rope ladder and managed to scale the wall just as the transport arrived.

But now his luck deserted him.

As he climbed down the ladder to freedom on the other side of the wall he was seized with cramp and tumbled to the ground. Before he could recover, he was recaptured.

On the same day, Tingley was retaken, this time at a public house in

Chailey. At the Lent Assizes at Horsham in March 1807, Tingley was acquitted of the robbery at Albourne but as he was wanted in Somerset on a charge of violent burglary, he was transferred there to stand trial. He was found guilty and hanged at Ilchester.

At Horsham, in March 1807, eight people were condemned to death. At the end of the Assizes, seven were reprieved. It was Bignall alone who awaited execution. He did not disclose the whereabouts of £400 he had accumulated from crime in the hope that a fellow prisoner in whom he had confided would tell his wife where the money was so that she and his children would be taken care of. Perhaps she did profit at the last although there is no record of it.

On 3 April, 1807, on his last night, Bob Bignall sent a letter to the Reverend Mr Marshall in which he wrote:

'And if, Sir, it is convenient for you to come tomorrow morning, I shall be happy to see you and my wife together.'

How calm and resigned he sounds.

To his family, his father, his wife and children, he wrote:

'When you receive this, I shall be no more – I have sinned and I have repented. So, adieu, my dear friends.'

The next day Bob Bignall made his stylish and dignified exit.

GLEANINGS 1802–1805

25 January 1802

The following robbery was committed on Thursday evening in the parish of Slaugham:– As Mr. Cremer, a master warrener, was without–side his house putting up his window shutters, he was accosted by two men who demanded of him whether any person was within his house. On his answering that could be no business of theirs, and asking whether they meant to rob him, one of them replied that they had come for that purpose, and instantly seizing him by the collar, dragged him into the house, and with presented pistols robbed him of forty pounds in cash.

29 March 1802

The Judge, during the trial of Rogers and Mongford, was pleased to applaud in the strongest terms of approbation, the establishment of our nightly patrol, through whose vigilance the felony with which the prisoners stood charged, was brought to light.

14 January 1805

The soldier in custody for stealing meat in a butcher's shop, was on Monday tried by a Court Martial and found guilty. He was the next morning punished with 450 lashes.

1 April 1805

At our Assize which ended at Horsham on Tuesday last, there were 29 prisoners for trial, 15 of whom were capitally convicted, and received sentence of death, viz. George Williams, aged 28, for stealing divers bridles and saddles, the property of different persons – Edward Byrne, aged 22, James Birmingham, 25, John Cole and John Stone, 19 years each, soldiers in the 88th Regiment, for sheep–stealing – William King, 64, also for sheep–stealing – William Harris, 49 years old, for a burglary in the dwelling house of John Tooth of East Grinstead – Ann Davis alias Gordon, aged 27, for the wilful murder of her new–born female infant – Samuel Harman, aged 14, for stealing in the dwelling house of Alexander Walker, three notes, value one pound each – John Bedwell, aged 39, for sheep–stealing –James Maidlow, aged 17, for a burglary in the house of James Wood – John Sacre, 55, for sheep–stealing – Sophia Turner, aged 18, for stealing a silver watch and seal, the property of Messrs. Levy and Yates – Thomas Piper, aged 25, for a burglary in the house of John Richardson of Withyham – and Mary Ann Bartholomew, aged 15, for feloniously stealing a £20 Lewes Bank Note, the property of her master, Mr. New of Ringmer.

The first named eight of the capital convicts are left for execution; the remaining seven were reprieved before the Judges left the town.

The unhappy young woman, for the murder of her bastard child, was to have suffered on Tuesday last, but it being represented to the Judge that her mind was in a state of distraction from the effects of her sentence, he humanely granted her a respite, until her mind should become more quiet, and she was better reconciled to her melancholy fate; but of this she betrays no symptoms, as her excessive perturbation continues, and shuts out all hope of consolation, and her death is, we hear, in consequence daily expected.

From the *Sussex Weekly Advertiser*

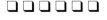

3

A MARESFIELD MYSTERY

AS if one hanging offence was not enough, Robert Bingham was charged with two. No wonder then that Horsham in March 1811 was crowded, that every room in every hostelry and decent lodging house was occupied and 'that several gentlemen were constrained to procure beds in neighbouring villages.' There had not been a case of such compelling interest at the Assizes for years.

The previous December, Richard Jenner, a Maresfield farmer, had received a letter which had alarmed him. Addressed to 'Mr Ri Jinner, Maresfield', misspelt and lacking punctuation, the letter read:

MURDER FIRE and REVENGE
Fifty of us are detarmd to keep our land or have revenge therefore
pason churchwards and farmers your barns and houses shall burn
if you take our land your lives two shall pay your sheep we will eat
your oxen we can mame your stacks shall blaze Dick you shall be
shuted as you comes from markt or fares we are United an are
sworn to stand biy one another.
FIFTY GOOD FELLOWS

Had one of the foresters, with whom the farmers and those with ancient common rights constantly battled, sent the letter? Ashdown Forest was for generations the scene of struggles over illegal enclosures, the erection of fences and hedges, the felling of trees. It would not be the first letter of that kind from one of the squatter families. In the past barns and stacks had been fired, sheep had been stolen, oxen had been maimed.

However, from the start there had been some unease about Robert Bingham. Was he, rather than some forester, the culprit?

The matter occasioned much concern among the eleven hundred inhabitants of the parish. Nor had it been resolved by 17 January when, in the early hours of the morning, the parsonage was burnt to the ground.

Again attention was focused on Bingham. Within a week of the fire he was arrested and charged with two capital offences – sending an anonymous letter containing threats and arson.

Small wonder then that the trial attracted so many visitors to Horsham, particularly as the well–connected Robert Bingham, forty three years of age, father of twelve, had been for the past six years curate of Maresfield. As the rector was an absentee, Bingham had sole charge of the parish and had earned golden opinions for his good works. Yet he was not universally loved for there were those who, anxious about liberalism, disapproved of his starting a charity school for the children of the lowest orders. He was correct and rigid in his attitude to morals and disliked by many of the foresters for criticising their behaviour. They thought him an interfering prig.

It was Richard Jenner's own children, John and Richard, and their cousin, William, who had found the letter. When they were on their way home from church on Sunday, 16 December, they heard a horseman calling out behind them that if they did not move he would run them down. They looked round and saw it was their curate and teacher, Robert Bingham, having a joke with them.

It was after he had ridden past that the boys found the letter in the road. On reaching home, John had given it to his mother. His father was away in London. After dinner Sarah Jenner visited her sister–in–law, the wife of Thomas Jenner, and showed her the letter. Both assumed it was written by a forester for who else would send such a disgraceful threat?

Richard Jenner and his wife had known the Binghams since the curate's arrival in the parish six years earlier. They were close neighbours, they had sent their three sons to be taught by him and the families were very friendly. It was perfectly natural for Sarah Jenner to show the letter to the Binghams on the Sunday evening.

The following Sunday, Richard Jenner having returned to Maresfield, he called on the curate to speak to him about the letter. It must have been a difficult meeting for him, for he had come to a different conclusion from his wife as to its authorship.

He was to tell the court: ' I thought it was his writing but thought he could not do it. I could not harbour the thought in my breast.'

The curate suggested that he visit the stationers' shops in the district to see who sold paper bearing the same watermark, 'Evans and Co 1806,' as the letter. The farmer followed this advice but found no shop selling such paper. He knew, however, that he had other letters and bills for school fees in the house bearing the tell-tale watermark and all of them were endorsed

'Ri Jenner', and were from Bingham.

At the trial, Jenner said he believed the threatening letter was in the curate's handwriting, slightly disguised. He was asked to identify any features he considered typical of the curate's hand. He indicated the 'Ri'; the shape of the R, the s and the b; the capital J looking like an unusual form of g; in Maresfield the letter f was formed without a loop at the bottom. And was there not something Biblical about the cadences of the note, even though it was not remarked on in court?

If you take our land your lives too shall pay. Your sheep we will eat. Your oxen we can maim. Your stacks shall blaze.

Is there the hint here of a literate man? If so, it was not argued in court but the style of the note as well as the formation of the letters might well have been responsible for lodging suspicion in some minds.

Jenner had tried to persuade himself that Bingham was innocent. At a meeting of the Prosecuting Society in December, attended by the farmer and the curate, it had been suggested that William Best, now in the Lewes House of Correction, might have had something to do with the letter. After all, he was there awaiting trial because Jenner had accused him of stealing hay.

Jenner visited Lewes to speak to Best but no progress was made. There was no convincing reason to think the man in any way responsible.

In court, Jenner's opinion that the handwriting was Bingham's was backed up by others. Several reliable villagers had had letters and bills from the curate and were equally convinced that the writing was his.

Then there was the curious remark which Bingham had made at a social gathering at the parsonage a day or so before Christmas. Jenner told the court that the clergyman had come out with the comment: 'Dick, you are not shooted yet.' A joke perhaps. But it discomfited the farmer.

The prosecuting counsel asked what Jenner's response had been.

A I said, by God, sir, if I had not so good an opinion of you as I have, I should have thought you had written that letter.

Q What did Mr. Bingham do?

A He turned his head away from me, and said, Aha! Aha!

Q Set up an affected laugh?

A He did.

Bingham addressed the court in his own defence. Young Jenner had told the court he had seen him drop the letter. If that was so why had the boy waited a month before telling anyone? It was sheer imagination. He had heard the matter spoken of so often that he had invented the scene. After

25

all, people had been talking about the letter for the last three months in all the little clubs and parties in the neighbourhood. But why, he asked, should he write such a note to his neighbours and friends? What could be his motive?

The curate hoped the jury would acquit him and restore him 'to society, to my profession, to the arms of my afflicted family, and the support of my innumerable children.'

The defence showed that there were local stationers' shops selling paper with the Evans watermark. It was not Bingham alone who had access to it. Richard Jenner had simply not made sufficient inquiries.

A number of influential people spoke in the curate's favour and Lord Sheffield sought to lay the blame elsewhere – on the enemies of the hard-working Bingham.

'In consequence of the disorders of the parish, and for curing those disorders, there is no person in the county that has been more diligent than he has been,' he said. 'A great many of the complaints that have been made in regard to public houses and different disorders that have been remedied have been a great deal of the cause of that rancour that has been shown against him. . . especially on account of his exertions to suppress the bad morals of the people called foresters in that neighbourhood. I found him more active than anybody in carrying into effect the instructions given at the Sessions.'

In the end no one could offer a convincing motive and it was this which persuaded the jury to acquit the curate on the first charge.

Bingham's second trial began immediately after the first one ended. The indictment boiled down to one of arson and attempting to defraud the Union Fire Society over the loss of furniture and personal belongings.

On the night of 16 January, the family and servants had gone to bed at about 9pm, the curate being the last to retire. At some stage he heard something outside and went downstairs to investigate. Finding nothing, he returned to bed. Some time after midnight, he again heard a noise. Again he went downstairs and out into the garden and saw in the road outside the unidentifiable figure of a man walking towards Maresfield Street. He searched the house and went back to the bedroom.

Had he looked in the schoolroom which adjoined the house, his wife asked him.

Bingham went downstairs once more but he was unable to get into the schoolroom from inside the house because the connecting door, as he was to find out, was barricaded on the other side. Going to the outside door to the schoolroom he saw that it had been forced open. Inside he saw smoke and flames coming from a table, a bench and some faggots with which the inner door had been barricaded.

He could have put out the fire with two or three buckets of water, he was to tell the court, but there was none to hand and the well was seventy five feet deep. He failed to explain satisfactorily why he had not sought some buckets and filled them from the pond next to the stable.

Bingham rushed upstairs to rouse his family and servants, sending twelve year old Thomas Caley to ring the church bells and to get help. By 1am the fire was raging violently and the schoolroom had already burnt down. People came from neighbouring houses to help but the fire had too strong a hold.

Bingham tried frantically to save what he could. He threw documents and papers out of windows, recovered £30 from a drawer in the school-room, manhandled a bed out of an upstairs window and had eventually to be called out of the blazing house. No man, said one witness, exposed himself more to save the furniture than he did. Later, when the walls had tumbled down, Bingham left the smoking ruin and went to Thomas Jenner's house where he and the family were to stay.

Richard Jenner said when he called in to see Bingham at breakfast time, he claimed he was a ruined man. All his effects were burned, except for what he had saved out of the ruins. His clothes and linen were worth between £100 and £150, his books £100, his furniture as much as £1,000. But he was insured for only £500. He wondered about his plate and watch which were later retrieved, but were badly damaged. Fortunately his family was safe. The nine children in the house had been hastily clothed and taken to the safety of The Chequers Inn, while he and his wife had striven to save what they could. But it was a short lived reprieve. Within days one of the children was to die from a chill contracted on the night of the fire.

It was in the next few days that doubts were once more raised.

The curate had recently increased his contents insurance from £450 to £500.

His behaviour the day before the fire had been unusual.

He had saved some of his possessions but he had not tackled the fire when he first saw it.

Papers had been found, buried or hidden in strange places.

Before Christmas he had transferred the parish registers from the parsonage to the church.

Lord Sheffield had been so alarmed by the conflagration that he insisted on professional police assistance. One of his employees, Joseph Adkins, had a brother, Henry, who was a Bow Street officer. He was sent for.

The court was to hear how the day before the fire, Bingham and young Caley had taken documents and papers out of the main house. Three dozen books had been discovered later, buried under a recently planted bush in the garden Some account books were found in the chicken house. A search of the stables revealed a collection of sermons.

Henry Adkins questioned Bingham about these matters on Monday, 21 January, and then continued his investigation of the parsonage ruins, grounds and outhouses.

The following day it was reported that the curate had been seen digging in the garden and had unearthed a parcel of books.

That evening Adkins returned to Thomas Jenner's house and told the curate he was dissatisfied with his answers of the previous day.

Why had Caley told him there was no barricade and that the fire was in the middle of the room?

Why, on the night before the fire, had Bingham told Caley to keep away from the chicken house?

What about these hidden papers?

And the stable – had it not been burnt down in October for which the insurance company had paid out £187 6s. 2d?

When Adkins told Bingham he was to be arrested, the clergyman asked him if he had a warrant. Adkins replied that he had, and went on:

'He says: "Now then I must submit." Immediately upon that he said: "If you will burn that warrant, I will give you all the information you want." I told him it would answer no purpose to burn the warrant as I could take him without it. He said he must submit again'.

Pressed about the buried books, Bingham became agitated but offered no sound reasons for his action.

Of course there were reasons, the defence claimed, for the curate's seemingly bizarre behaviour. At the root of it lay his anxiety that his house was to be burned down. Had not the threatening letter mentioned the parson? It was for this reason that the parish registers had been taken from the parsonage and lodged in the church. Explaining the increase in insurance, the secretary of Union Fire said that letters had been sent and that the curate was under considerable alarm that his house would be destroyed. The increase of premium was only another £50 and well short of complete cover.

As for Caley's evidence, according to the defence, it was worthless. The boy had been reprimanded for lying in the past by his master.

Again addressing the jury, Bingham asked if it seemed reasonable for him to burn down the house, to risk his family's lives, to deprive them of their home. He was not in debt and had a well furnished house. What was to be gained for he was lamentably under–insured? The fire had cost him dear.

Robert Bingham left the court a free man. Two crimes had been committed. By whom? A forester with a grudge? A man called Goldspring blamed Bingham for having been refused a licence to sell beer. Was it Goldspring then? Or even Best, soon to be out of the House of Correction, acquitted of the charge that Jenner had brought against him? Or had it been someone else?

Or could it possibly have been Bingham himself who wrote that letter, with its faint echoes of the scriptures? Could the curate have laid that furious fire?

REV. Mr. BINGHAM's TRIAL,

At the SUSSEX ASSIZES, before the
LORD CHIEF BARON.

On Saturday next, will be published,
BY W. AND A. LEE,
Price 2s. 6d.

THE TRIAL, AT LARGE,

OF THE
Rev. ROBERT BINGHAM,

Charged, on suspicion, of having feloniously and unlawfully sent a threatening Letter, without a Name subscribed thereto, to Mr. RICHARD JENNER, of Maresfield:
And also, on suspicion of having feloniously and maliciously set Fire to a Dwelling House, then in his possession, at Maresfield, &c. &c.

As taken at Horsham, on Tuesday, the 26th of March, 1811,
BY J. V. BUTTON, B. A.

☞ Orders for the above, very interesting Trial, will be received at the OFFICES of the PUBLISHERS, at LEWES; or by their several NEWSCARRIERS, throughout the County.

Even in 1811 accounts of major trials were of great public interest, as this advertisement shows.

But if so, why? It is a mystery. With so many questions unanswered.

A mystery indeed, especially in view of what then happened to Bingham and his family. He was replaced by another clergyman instead of being reinstated to the post in which he had served with such distinction.

Was there some public pressure which eased him out?

Did the Church suspect, even know of, some unrevealed matters?

Robert Bingham had been acquitted so why should he leave Maresfield?

For he was innocent.

Was he not?

GLEANINGS 1807–1810

19 January 1807

John Luck, convicted of feloniously stealing one gander and two geese, the property of Mr. John Shoesmith of Heathfield, and of violent behaviour when apprehended, was sentenced to seven years' transportation to such parts beyond the seas as His Majesty, by the advice of His Privy Council, shall think fit and direct.

28 March 1807

William Ball, the unfortunate young man who at our last Summer Assizes was found guilty of forgery on the Bank of England, and whose judgment was respited, in consequence of an exception which in point of law had been taken, was brought to the bar, and informed that his case had been submitted to the opinion of the Judges, whose decision was that his conviction was right. The dreadful sentence of the law was then pronounced against him, which he heard with firmness, and in a manner highly becoming one in his unhappy situation. The debt due to the offended laws of his country will be cancelled with his life on next Saturday se'n-night, at the fatal tree, and we may venture to assert amid the commiserations of all present.

17 September 1810

The unfortunate convict, Wilson, who was executed on Saturday the 8th inst. at Horsham for a burglary in the shop of Mr. Gill, watchmaker, at Rye, wrote a letter a few days prior to his execution to Mr. Gill, informing him in the most solemn manner, that he had given three of the stolen watches, all new ones, to a Corporal of the regiment to which he belonged; two to Privates, and that two others were hid in a wall at Winchelsea; he also stated that an accomplice named Hodges had all the rest of the stolen property with which he deserted soon after the commission of the robbery.

In consequence of this information, Mr. Gill went to Dover where the regiment then was and endeavoured to recover some of his property; but the parties accused by the letter of the convict denied ever having had the watches; and all he has been able to recover is two, one or both of which have been found in the wall at Winchelsea.

From the *Sussex Weekly Advertiser*

4

THREE AND A HALF DOZEN PIGEONS

WHAT was it that persuaded poor, foolish Jesse Attree to take such ridiculous risks? He was thirty five, married with a young family and in regular work as a blacksmith at Hollebone's forge at Firle. Of course, any man might go poaching and Jesse Attree certainly did that. In spite of the severe Game Laws, nothing could persuade country dwellers that what they were doing was wrong. After all, there were such things as natural rights.

It was not the poaching but his other offences that incline one to think the blacksmith foolish for although they were not particularly wicked they were committed against the most powerful man in the district.

Attree's folly was compounded one early summer's day in 1815 when he went to Seaford and got drunk. On his way home across the Downs, accompanied by Thomas Howard, a seventy year old labourer, Attree was in an expansive and confiding mood. Firle might be Lord Gage's village, he told his companion. He might own all the land and all the houses for miles around, but Jesse Attree knew something that Lord Gage did not.

Howard was an eager listener as Attree boasted that during the previous winter he had broken into Lord Gage's pigeon house several times and had helped himself to a number of birds.

Ah yes, Attree had said in reply to the obvious question, the pigeon house had been locked. But was he not a blacksmith? Did not blacksmiths make and repair keys?

Another night, Attree went on, he and young William Kennard had gone to the pigeon house and had taken three and a half dozen birds. These they had taken 'to a man who occasionally carried letters for Tinsley the regular postman and who is usually called the Pieman'.

In fact, Attree confided, he kept the key hidden in the stable at Place Farm where another of his accomplices, Samuel Horscraft, worked as groom. The farm was only a short distance from where the elegant brick and flint pigeon house stood in a field. Each of the men had access to the key and they could go there whenever they liked.

Attree must never have stopped talking on the walk from Seaford to

Firle. He told Howard that he had the key to the wine cellar at Place Farm and he could go there whenever he liked, he bragged – though not totally truthfully – and help himself to the choice wines belonging to John Ellman, a member of one of the county's most influential farming families.

Then there were the night time trips into the grounds of Firle Place, Lord Gage's mansion in the heart of the village, where Attree and his friends fished the pond. They would sell some of their catch in Brighton where two of his brothers worked in taverns which were always ready to buy game and fish, no questions asked. Wealthy landowners dining out expected to eat well and they would often find on their plates illegally obtained fish and flesh, sometimes from their own estates.

Howard was intrigued by what he had heard. Some days later he brought up the subject with Kennard who told him that 'he had taken eels out of the Garden Pond, one of which weighed a pound'.

Men do not usually confide in those they do not trust. In the case of Thomas Howard, however, the trust that Attree and Kennard placed in him was misplaced for the old man sought out James Fuller, Lord Gage's assistant gamekeeper, who passed him on to Thomas Budgen, the head keeper. He had some information, he said.

The information, however, was not enough for Budgen. Even in those days men could not be taken into custody on hearsay evidence so Howard was asked to provide more substantial proof. He would have to join the men when they entered the pigeon house, be with them when they laid lines in the pond and when they went after rabbits and hares. This was quite an undertaking for a man of his age, yet he consented.

One evening he visited the Garden Pond with Kennard to see if the others had laid any lines. As they had not and as Kennard had not brought any with him, the trial proceedings relate that 'they got over the iron gate at the head of the pond into the garden and searched the frames for cucumbers whilst the said William Kennard took out five or six cucumbers, the informant (Thomas Howard) taking two for his share and the said William Kennard the remainder.'

On another occasion Howard was shown by Kennard where the key to the pigeon house was kept. They failed, however, to budge the lock and therefore left empty-handed. Some weeks later Howard went with Attree to fish Lord Gage's pond. They put out eighteen lines and caught nothing so after two hours they left.

These men do seem to have experienced so many failures that the worthwhileness of their ventures must be in doubt. Were they obsessed by

The pigeon house at Firle as it is today. Photo: Julian Tayler

the sport of it or were they desperate for food and money?

On 1 August, after only a few weeks as a member of Attree's gang, Howard had enough evidence to satisfy Budgen and an application was made to the magistrates for an arrest warrant. Lord Gage's bailiff, Joseph Richards, swore on oath that three dozen pigeons had been stolen the previous winter, stating that he suspected the offence had been committed by Jesse Attree, William Kennard and Samuel Horscraft. Some days later, he added Henry Kennard, William's cousin, to his list. This man's name appeared several times in Horscraft's statement but no firm proof from any reliable witness was ever offered against him.

William Clark, 'who saith that he hath under him the care of the pigeon house of Lord Viscount Gage', was interviewed. He said that although he had the previous winter suspected that birds were being stolen he could not be sure how many had gone because of their great number. However, he gave a clear indication of how the men had been able to enter the pigeon house.

'He well remembered,' he said 'that the lock of the pigeon house went to be repaired at the shop of Charles Hollebone of Firle, Blacksmith, and he believed that the same was altered or repaired by Jesse Attree there who is one of the workmen of the said Charles Hollebone.'

The story of the theft of the pigeons was pieced together from Howard's statement and the subsequent evidence of the letter-carrier George Tinsley, from Abraham Worsell, 'the Pieman', and from Samuel Horscraft whose confession was made shortly after his arrest. The latter, father of two girls, the elder not yet two years old, succumbed to pressure and gave a full account of his part in the offences and consequently escaped punishment.

Horscraft's confession first described how Attree came by Ellman's key. The blacksmith had been called to Place Farm on legitimate business to ease the lock of a drawer. There he had seen a bunch of keys, one of which, either because it was labelled or because he had earlier worked on it, he recognised as the cellar key.

Two days later Attree had taken a bundle of picklock keys to Horscraft's stable. One of them would unlock the cellar, he told the groom.

The next morning, before his master had come downstairs and 'whilst the maids were gone to milk the cows', Horscraft went down to the cellar and stole a bottle of white wine. He hid it in a chest in the stable and when Attree called in the evening, they drank it together.

Ellman's cellar was not entered again, however, for when Attree urged him to go after another bottle, Horscraft refused. Presumably he understood the folly of his action, the risk he had taken, the consequences of discovery, the potential effect on his wife and children. Thus, Attree's boast to Howard which implied that he had regular access to the cellar seems to have been exaggerated.

But Attree was involved in other activities. During the winter he had made himself another key, this time to the parish coal hole where fuel for the poor was stored. In the terrible winter of 1814–1815, money was short and many families in dire need were grateful for free coal doled out by the Overseers of the Poor.

Attree, although employed, must have felt himself entitled to a share but like most of his petty offences, it was surely not worth the risk.

Horscraft gave accounts of forays into the pigeon house when they would come away with half a dozen birds. On at least one occasion, not having an oven in his cottage, he took his birds to be cooked by the local baker.

Another time he said he was accompanied by Henry Kennard. That night, the young groom claimed, Kennard took nineteen birds, stuffing them down his smock which was tied at the waist with string. The two men went back to Kennard's cottage where one of the birds wriggled down his sleeve and escaped via the slit in the cuff. Kennard managed to catch the bird and killed it. He pushed it back in his smock where the remaining birds were still lodged. This graphic story tends to confirm one's belief in Henry Kennard's involvement in the thefts.

As the inquiries proceeded, George Tinsley and Abraham Worsell, both Lewes men, were called in for questioning by the magistrates.

Worsell told how one evening Attree and William Kennard had arrived at his house with a sackful of pigeons. He had not wanted the birds, explaining that he thought they might have been stolen, but he agreed to take his visitors to Tinsley's house for, as the organiser of pigeon shooting matches, Tinsley often bought pigeons.

The four men went to the White Lion and bought drinks. Tinsley explained how he very reluctantly took four pigeons as a gift but he could not say what happened to the remainder of the birds.

Worsell's recall of this meeting was vague and selective. He could not say what agreement Tinsley had reached with the men from Firle. He had an idea that Tinsley had taken a dozen birds which he had sold, some for sixpence and others for fourpence But he could not remember to whom they had been sold. Nor could he bring to mind how Attree had got rid of the remainder.

But both Attree and Kennard were to claim that Worsell had bought some pigeons and Worsell was charged with receiving.

The Calendar of Persons in Lewes House of Correction to be brought before the Court of General Quarter Sessions on 20th October, 1815 included Jesse Attree.

He was charged on the oath of Joseph Richards of Firle and also on the confession of Samuel Horscraft, an accomplice, with 'having in company together lately broken open and entered the pigeon house of the Right Honourable Lord Viscount Gage at the parish of Firle and feloniously stole twelve pigeons.'

William Kennard and Attree were further charged with the theft of three and a half dozen pigeons. Both men were found guilty and were each transported for seven years. Worsell was acquitted of receiving, the jury being disinclined to bring in a guilty verdict for this kind of offence on the testimony of a confessed offender.

Howard, whose evidence had led to the arrest of the offenders, died at Firle in 1819. Samuel Horscraft moved to the neighbouring village of Berwick. On the expiry of his sentence, Jesse Attree returned to Firle and took up his work as a blacksmith again. He died and was buried there in 1851. There is no indication about what happened to William Kennard although his cousin Henry, who had on this occasion escaped charges, was transported in 1826 for the theft of a bushel of potatoes. He too returned to Firle, dying in the workhouse there in 1882.

Was it worth it? All for a sack of pigeons.

GLEANINGS 1811–1813

22 April 1811

Last Wednesday Mary Dennis and Mary Richardson, her daughter, were committed to the House of Correction at Lewes, charged with stealing in the shop of Mr. Bodle in Alfriston, about 80 yards of ribbon of different sorts, in rolls, the greatest part of which, in searching them, was found concealed under the peak of their stays.

Brighton Gazette 2 July 1812

Whereas in the evening of Sunday the 28th June last, or early the next morning, the stable belonging to Mr. Wm. Blunden, situate in the parish of Goring, adjoining to Clapham Common, in the county of Sussex, was entered by some person or persons and a BLACK GIG HORSE, with a bridle and saddle, were stolen thereout, but the horse has since been found loose on the Common. Whoever will give information of the offender or offenders, so that he or they may be brought to Justice, shall on conviction receive a reward of Three Guineas, to be paid out of the funds of the Lancing Society for Prosecuting Thieves and Other Offenders, and a further reward of One Guinea from Mr. Blunden.

From the Sussex Weekly Advertier

5

THE SHIPLEY GANG

WHAT a contrast to the foolish men of Firle were the members of the Shipley gang – the most active and most violent lawbreakers in the area round Horsham immediately after the Napoleonic Wars.

In this period of agricultural recession crime increased as a consequence of high bread prices, low wages and unemployment. Many of the offences were petty – thefts of chickens, bags of flour, wood – although when the perpetrators were caught they faced an uncertain range of punishments for the sentencing was frequently haphazard. One man might hang, another might find himself in the House of Correction for a couple of years for the same offence, yet another might be 'boated' to New South Wales for a minimum of seven years.

Crime flourished through the lack of any effective law enforcement. It was the resistance to the establishment of a professional police force, seen as an infringement of an Englishman's rights, that made it difficult to prevent crime. So the Shipley gang, and others like it, prospered while the law-abiding citizens awaited visits from them with terror.

The gang was led by James Rapley, a hardened offender sometimes known as 'Robin Hood', whose sons, James and Daniel, joined him in his enterprises. Other members of the gang included William Browne, James Jupp, James Ewens, James Nye senior and James Nye junior, Thomas Tilley and Henry Mitchell. From time to time, they were joined by others but in the main, the Shipley gang, quartered in Southwater Woods, was a group of full time thieves. They were professionals.

From their woodland base they stole sheep, broke into houses, forced their way into mills. They stole from outhouses, barns and shops. Over the two or three years of their major activity, they went off with a considerable amount of loot. The cottages they occupied were treasure houses containing sacks of grain, jackets, carcases of sheep, lengths of linen, food, farm tools – a grand miscellany of stolen goods.

The gang numbered a dozen or so, several of them with dependants, so that to make a living for such a large number they had to be increasingly active and undeniably desperate.

There were outlets for the goods they stole. Clothing was sold in markets and shops with no questions asked and tools were got rid of in the same way. Not every miller and brewer asked where grain came from, not every baker was scrupulous about the flour he bought. Only from a regular, uninterrupted career of theft, on a large scale, with a reliable network of receivers, could so large a gang survive.

In the surrounding parishes nothing, it seems, was safe. In groups of up to five they descended, often on horseback, on frightened farmers, shopkeepers and householders in Nuthurst, Shermanbury, West Chiltington, Rudgwick, Horsham, Ashurst, Thakeham, Billingshurst, Rowhook, Broadbridge Heath.

Some of the crimes are known about but there were countless others of which there is no record. The reputation of the Shipley gang would be slight if it were to rely solely on the cases which came up at their trial at Horsham Assizes in 1818.

To some extent, they were politic, in that they left alone the properties in their own parish. No trembling Shipley shoemaker or grocer acting as parish constable was obliged to call on them to put questions, to ask to search their homes, to arrest them. Drunken farm lads were trouble enough for parish constables but the Shipley gang would have presented a different kind of duty.

Yet taking only one or two of the gang would have availed little. There can be little doubt that unless the whole gang were under arrest or in some way dispersed, any witnesses would be threatened. Farmers who wished to volunteer information would fear for their barns, for their winter stocks, for their animals. Until 1817 when the principal members were captured and they were brought to trial, there is no indication of any member of the Shipley gang being charged and imprisoned.

Did they really throw a potential witness in a lime pit? Did they really threaten to drown a man at Gosden Mill? Perhaps not. But these were good enough stories to be circulated around the surrounding communities. Who would wish to oppose such desperadoes?

Eventually some people decided that enough was enough. A parish constable named Hammond gathered up a sufficient number of like minded fellows, determined to put an end to the continuing law breaking.

One night after a successful robbery and intending to share their stolen property, the gang met at a cottage at the bottom of Bonfire Hill in Southwater. Hammond placed men at the rear of the cottage and on a signal they burst in through the rear door. The gang members promptly fled through the front door where Hammond waited with a club in his hands. However, in the ensuing melee every one of them escaped.

In August 1817, a similar attempt was made to apprehend the gang, this time at Wedge's Farm, Itchingfield, where thirteen bushels of flour from Rudgwick mill had been hidden in the outbuildings ready to be moved on. This time the constables and their volunteer helpers were successful. James Rapley, the leader, was arrested along with James Ewens, Philip Jupp and his son Henry, and the two Nyes.

But not all the gang were captured at Wedge's Farm and immediately, reward notices were published, one in the *Sussex Weekly Advertiser* of 25 August 1817, pictured below, giving the only available descriptions of the wanted men.

James Jupp and Daniel Rapley were soon taken. The younger James Rapley continued his criminal career for some months before he was arrested. Sarah Rapley did not come into the story again. Perhaps she was not directly responsible for any offence.

The following week the newspaper reported that 'James Rapley senior was on Tuesday morning last, found in his shirt, hanging by a half handkerchief fastened to the window bars of his cell in the Petworth House of Correction. . .'

After viewing the body in the gaol, 'G. Gwynne, Esq., and the Jury, composed half of Prisoners and half of others, returned a Verdict of Insanity.'

The charges which the gang faced at their trial could not easily have been proved without two of

Housebreakers and Thieves fled from Justice.

Js. Rapley, jun.
Daniel Rapley
Middle size, light hair and complexion; one about 27 years of age, the other 23, usually dressed in light brown round jackets with sleeves.

Sarah Rapley,
Middle size, light hair and complexion, 20 years old, plain, but decently dressed.

James Jupp,
Near 6 feet high, light complexion, a little freckled, sandy hair cut short, about 23 years of age, turns his toes out more than labourers in general, dressed usually in a dark round frock, and has passed as husband to Sarah Rapley.

All four belong to the Parish of Shipley.

N. B. There being Warrants out against them, all Persons are desired to take before a Justice persons resembling their descriptions, who cannot give a good account of themselves, informing the Clerk to the Magistrates of Horsham of their being in Custody, forthwith.

The Rewards for their apprehension will, on conviction, be considerable.

the accused, Thomas Tilley and Henry Mitchell, both of whom in the customary way, in return for their freedom, gave evidence for the Crown.

William Browne, James Ewens, Henry and James Jupp, the two Nyes, and Daniel Rapley were sentenced to death, but this was commuted to fourteen years' transportation. James Rapley junior was later transported for a similar term. Philip Jupp, whose two sons were 'boated', was given six months' hard labour in Petworth House of Correction for the theft of a fork.

How the helpless communities in the vicinity of Southwater Woods must have sighed with relief at the break up of the Shipley gang. Yet not for another twenty years would they have a policeman. Petty, irritating crime would go on and it would be hard to prevent but nothing on the scale of the reign of terror inflicted by James Rapley and his followers on the neighbourhood would ever occur again..

GLEANINGS 1815–1817

8 May 1815

Last Saturday thirteen deserters from the Duke of Wellington's Army, while on service in the Peninsula, who had been given up by Louis XVIII, after being landed at Rye, were escorted by a strong officer's guard of the 58th Regiment, handcuffed to a rope like felons going to trial,on their march to the Depot at the Isle of Wight; we suppose in order to be sent to condemned Regiments in the West Indies, the properest situation for them, as some appeared to be desperate fellows, and betrayed strong symptoms of mutiny.

15 August 1815

James West, aged 18, convicted of feloniously stealing a silver watch, value 40/-, the property of Henry Peters of Wiston, was sentenced to transportation for the term of his natural life.

23 December 1816

A few days since William Hards, James Hards and Uriah Milton were committed to the House of Correction for being found in a certain wood, called Welland Wood, in the parish of Ewhurst, with gun and other instruments for the purpose and with an intention of killing and destroying game.

21 April 1816

John Ayling, for stealing a faggot of wood, of the value of twopence, the property of John Sargent, Esq., of Woolavington and Edward Legatt for stealing at Eastergate, one faggot of wood, the property of Francis Bine. Each, one month's solitary confinement on bread and water.

11 August 1817

The tribe of BLACK LEGS, who are generally in the secret, anticipating the event of these Races, did not honour the turf with their accustomed visit; but the LIGHT FINGERED corps were in full attendance. On Wednesday they had a grand field day and practised their various manoeuvres, for the most part successfully. Several persons had their pockets picked of their watches, and others of their money, to the facility of which the tragic conflict between MR PUNCH, his consort JUDY and the DEVIL, in no small degree contributed, by fixing the attention of the crowd which the exhibition occasionally collected. A smart looking boy, only 14 years old (no doubt from London), was detected by Mr. Joshua Mantell, in picking the pocket of Edward Collbran, a butcher, of Southover. This young offender was fully committed for trial at the Assizes. Four one pound bank notes were found upon him, and to account for the possession of the same, he said the notes were the produce of oranges and lemons which he had sold; but this and other of his assertions were proved to be falsehoods.

1 December 1817

At Battle Fair, on Saturday se'nnight, three persons were taken up on suspicion of circulating counterfeit shillings and sixpences of the late coinage, but nothing being found on them to warrant their detention, they were dismissed. The principal and supposed cashier of this little band had contrived to get off before the others were taken up. Similar frauds were attempted but, we believe, without much success at Hastings Fair on the following Tuesday.

From the *Sussex Weekly Advertiser*

MILTON FIRE.

Near Alfriston.

£200. REWARD.

WHEREAS
On SUNDAY EVENING last,

THE

BARNS

AND RICKS,

At Milton Farm, in the Parish of Arlington,

Were maliciously SET on FIRE.

Whoever will give Information against the Offender or Offenders, so that he or they may be brought to Justice, shall receive TWO HUNDRED POUNDS -REWARD, over and above all other Rewards ; to be paid on Conviction.

F. H. GELL.

LEWES, 12th December, 1831.

BAXTER, PRINTER, LEWES.

6

ARSON AT ALFRISTON

ON the evening of 11 December, 1831, a barn was set on fire at Milton Court Farm, just over the river from Alfriston. So fierce was the blaze that within fifteen minutes the three floors of the building had collapsed and the roof had fallen in. Thirty six quarters of wheat, 150 quarters of barley, twenty quarters of peas and three haystacks were consumed.

This was not the first such fire in the neighbourhood. These were harsh and bitter years when some farm labourers, their conditions ever worsening, sought revenge on those they held responsible for their plight. It was a time, too, when drunken young men with aimless folly lit their way to waiting scaffolds. Throughout the south, farmers, many of them struggling in a wretched economic situation, saw their barns destroyed, their threshing machines, their winter hay, their ricks, their grain, reduced to ash.

Nor had Alfriston's other farmers escaped. In November 1830, Berwick Court Farm had suffered a costly fire. In the following October, the parsonage barn, next to the church, had been attacked with severe consequences. It was rented by two farmers, John Bodle and William Read. The former's property, according to the *Sussex Weekly Advertiser's* report of the incident 'consisted of 30 quarters of oats, 8 quarters of summer tares, a large quantity of straw and a new waggon, and the property belonging to Mr. Read consisted of 130 bushels of potatoes, some farming tackle and a quantity of straw. . .Had the wind been in the North East, the Church and National School must have fallen sacrifice to the flames. From the intense heat many panes of glass in the Church windows were broken.'

No one was brought to trial for these or any previous local fires. It was incidents of this kind which led the vicar, Charles Bohun Smith, to declare, 'The Devil is in this place' and for Ann Marchant, the saddler's wife, to write to her sister about alarming disorder and to refer to the village as 'this hateful place'.

However, within days this time, those responsible for the Milton Court fire were under arrest. At the time rural policing rested in the hands of the parish vestry and the prevention of crime and its detection relied on unskilled, unpaid, part time constables. But there were strong suspicions about who was to blame on this occasion and they were conveyed by Charles Ade, who farmed Milton Court, to the agent of the landlord, the Earl of Plymouth, who reacted swiftly. He summoned a detective from the newly formed Metropolitan Police.

Within four days of the fire, Detective Joseph Ticehurst's inquiries had led him to John Reeds, a farm labourer, who had already served time for the theft of grain and who had more recently escaped conviction for poisoning a foal on a nearby farm.

Ticehurst made it plain to Reeds that he had convincing evidence of what had occurred on the previous Sunday evening, warning him that if charged he would undeniably be found guilty and if guilty, hanged. Reeds determined to save himself, offering to act as chief prosecution witness. He named his friend, Samuel Thorncraft, as the man Ticehurst ought to speak to and advised the detective to search the cottage of Samuel Miller, Thorncraft's brother-in-law. Here Ticehurst found a tinderbox with steel, flint, a small piece of deal and a scallop shell in which brimstone had been melted.

Thorncraft, a twenty-two year old, had been employed by Ade for several years. He was not the best of workers and occasionally took time off to go drinking. At the trial a witness referred to the accused man being in Banks' beer shop in North Street in Alfriston when he ought to have been at work, just days before the fire. As his master rode by, Thorncraft had ducked down out of sight. Yet in spite of his imperfections as an employee, he had continued in Ade's employ over at least five years. Reeds, too, at the time of his arrest seems to have been employed by Ade, in spite of his bad record which must have been common knowledge.

Some years earlier, Ade – described by the *Brighton Gazette* as 'a most respectable farmer, who has ever proved himself the poor man's friend' – had prosecuted Thorncraft for the theft of seven apples and the seventeen year old had gone to prison for a month. He had served another month as the prime mover in a disturbance in the village centre when a huge bonfire threatened nearby houses.

In November, only weeks before the fire at Milton Court, Ade had taken Thorncraft before a magistrate in Lewes, accusing him of stealing six sacks of wheat. He could provide no evidence, however, to support his accusation and the charge was not proceeded with. In the succeeding weeks, the young labourer was to complain about how unjustly treated he had been in this matter.

After examination at Lewes in December 1831, Thorncraft confessed to having fired the barn at Milton Court but claimed that the idea had been put to him by John Reeds who was 'always drawing it into his head'. At the time he had been drunk, he said, otherwise he would never have burnt his master's property. Mr Ade had always been good to him, he assured his interrogators. Thorncraft was tried at Lewes Assizes in March 1832.

'The prisoner is an exceedingly fine made man,' the *Brighton Gazette* informed its readers, 'and his jet black hair and whiskers, with a scowling eye, and a determined and resolute appearance rendered him an object of much attention.'

Asked how he pleaded, the accused man answered 'that he wished to be tried by the laws of his country to see if he could be proved guilty'. The question was again put to him but he remained silent.

The case against Thorncraft was overwhelmingly strong. Several witnesses claimed to have heard him make incriminating remarks. Charles Smith told the court that in the early hours of 12 December, when efforts were still being made to fight the fire, he had talked to Thorncraft at the Royal Oak. If Ade asked why he was not helping to fight the fire, Thorncraft had said to Smith, 'he would d——d soon tell him'.

Sarah Young had heard Thorncraft speak against his employer several times when he was drunk. 'Some time before the fire', but she could not say how long before, she heard the prisoner say he did not care 'if Mr. Ade turned him away – if his master turned him away he would set every bloody building he had alight'.

On another occasion, Thorncraft had told fifteen year old William Weller, who worked with him, that he had not stolen his master's wheat, that he had been falsely accused and that 'he would pay Mr. Ade off for it'.

There had been talk that Ade intended to dismiss Thorncraft. With some show of bravado, Thorncraft had boasted to the tailor, James Young: 'Mr. Ade knows better than to discharge me'.

And had he been expressing an opinion based on personal experience when one day, talking about the buildings at Milton Court, he said to Michael Winchester, another workmate, 'If anybody set fire to that corner of the barn it would soon devour the lot'?

It was in the Royal Oak that James Young saw Thorncraft show Mercy Cox the steel he had won from Joseph Ford in a friendly wrestling match. He had said to her: 'I don't care as long as you don't get that for that is what I set the barns and hovels on fire with.' Was Thorncraft serious or was he joking, bragging or confessing his responsibility for other fires?

It was here, too, that the young man was heard to sing the doggerel lines with their reference to Stanton Collins, the local hero who was awaiting trial at Lewes Assizes for a series of robberies from farms.

Collins is merry there
And we be merry here
And set the barns
About their ears.

Reeds told the court what had led up to the fire and he described the eventual commission of the crime. On the Saturday night, the two men had been at Levett's beershop in Milton Street from eight o'clock until eleven. They were drunk when they returned to Thorncraft's house where they slept. By ten o'clock the next morning they were drinking once more at Levett's. Some time in the afternoon they went across to the Royal Oak at Lullington and on the way there Thorncraft told Reeds, apparently not for the first time, that if his master dismissed him, he would fire his barn. Then, after drinking more beer, he went outside.

Reeds' evidence continued: 'About four I went out and found the prisoner in the high road. He said, "Have you a mind to go?"

'I said, "I don't care."

'He asked if I had got the tinder and flint. I said "yes, I got father's unknown to him".

'Prisoner said he had got a flint. He went to his sister's and got a bunch of matches: we went over to Brig Meadow and across to Milton barn, and when there, went into the ox-stall which was fastened with a catch; prisoner opened the door; I struck a light; he lit the matches and told me to be off and I went away; he came after me and said it would not catch; he said he would go down to his sister's and get some more tinder, matches and a piece of candle; when there he said he wanted some tinder; she said she had not got any but she could make some.

'Samuel Miller (Thorncraft's brother-in-law) then went upstairs and fetched a box; prisoner then took the tinder out and put it on a piece of paper; he asked for matches; she said she had not got any more; she said she would make some; she then got a piece of wood; she and the prisoner cut some like other matches; she dipped the matches into the scallop shell in which there was melted brimstone; the prisoner asked for a piece of candle but I did not see it given him.'

But the Millers? Did they not pause to ask why they were being asked for these items? Was this usual? Did they not even for a moment ask why two half-drunk young men had called on them with such requests? Presumably the Millers had heard Samuel's boasts and threats. Did they not for one moment suspect what was in his mind?

Thorncraft and Reeds separated at this point and did not meet again until about seven o'clock. In the intervening two or three hours, they had not rethought their plan, had not dismissed it as a foolhardy product of their drinking. At seven o'clock, they were as resolute as they had been several hours earlier.

Reeds tells how he met Thorncraft again: 'It was near the Royal Oak; the prisoner and I went over the green meadow; we went towards Alfriston as far as the ash tree; we then went across to the barn; prisoner told me he had got tinder, matches and candle; we both went in at the stall; I struck the light; he lit the matches and told me to be off.

'I went away. I saw him put the matches in the peas mow; I went over to the rick settle; prisoner came after me and told me it had caught; we then ran across the green meadow; he told me he had the steel of J. Ford; he said he had got plenty of witnesses to show that it was Ford's steel; we went across the green field; I could not keep up with him so he stopt for me on the causeway. He said then, "Now we must go back", but we did not but ran across a ploughed field and lay in a hedge. We stopt a minute; he said, "we must not stop here or they will say it is us", so we ran back to the fire as far as we could and he got there first. I stopped there all night.'

Reeds implies that he busied himself helping to douse the flames. Thorncraft seems not to have given any assistance at the blaze and hours later, at two in the morning, still at the Royal Oak, he was assuring Charles Smith of the response he would give his employer if he was asked why he was not fighting the fire.

Some time during the evening or the early hours of morning he had sought out Joseph Ford. 'That's yours, I believe,' he had said, taking the steel out of his pocket and offering it to its owner.

Thorncraft had had it in mind on the night of the fire to implicate Joseph Ford. Reeds referred to that in his evidence. Ade's claim that Thorncraft had stolen some sacks of wheat had apparently resulted from information given by Ford. Exactly how Thorncraft's possession of Ford's steel and his later return of it would prove the latter's guilt is unclear.

Thorncraft was found guilty as charged. His father, John, standing up in court with tears in his eyes, implored the judge to forgive his son. 'He would send him thousands and thousands of miles away, never to do so any more, as he had an opportunity of getting him taken to America.'

A useless plea, as the *Brighton Gazette* reports: 'The judge then putting on the fatal black cap, in a very impressive and solemn manner pronounced the sentence of death, observing that the prisoner had been found guilty of a most heinous offence which crime, if suffered to escape the severity of the law, would render the habitation of man no longer a place of safety; that his case had been aggravated by a long-concealed malignity. His lordship then informed the prisoner that he could hope for no mercy on this side of the grave, and exhorted him to devote the remaining period of his existence to the duties of religion.'

Thorncraft's demeanour throughout the trial is said to have been calm and dignified. Only once did he call out to accuse one of the witnesses of lying. His only other recorded comment is that which he made to John Reeds at the end of the trial. Several in the court, including some of the women who had testified against him, had pressed forward and shaken his hand. Only when John Reeds offered his hand did Thorncraft refuse with the words that 'he would rather be tucked up here than tell as many lies as he had told'.

Whatever we may think of Reeds, and his record is not good, his account of what occurred on 11 December must be broadly true. He does not deny, could not deny, his part in what happened at Milton Court barn. But to find Reeds on the side of those who would hang him was undoubtedly difficult for Thorncraft to stomach.

In the meantime, there was some feeling of relief in the locality after the arrests of so many lawbreakers, even if only three suffered punishment. Mrs Ann Marchant, in a letter to her sister Mrs Sophie Peskett on 8 January 1832, wrote of her relief at the change in events.

'We were dreadfully alarmed with the fires and have no doubt but the greater part of Alfriston would have been consumed before the winter had ended had they not been arrested in their progress as they seemed bent on destruction.'

Thorncraft was hanged at Horsham on 3 April 1832. Typically the newspaper reports concentrate on the consolations he found in his religion so that 'he never indulged in the slightest hope of escape from the awful end that awaited him but evinced the greatest firmness and fortitude and paid the utmost attention to the religious instruction which was constantly administered to him by the Revd. Mr. Witherby, the worthy chaplain of the gaol'.

On the morning of his execution, Thorncraft's parents and his brother-in-law, Samuel Miller, visited him. The *Sussex Advertiser* devotes much space to the harrowing occasion. It reports that Thorncraft, composed throughout, assured his visitors that he was prepared for death and did not fear it. He expressed regrets for his past behaviour, blaming drink for his present plight. His parents were to ensure that his brothers did not follow the path he had taken.

After his execution, Thorncraft's parents took the body back to Alfriston in a cart for burial. Their son had ended up as yet another of those examples to others which had no effect.

The fires went on down the century, extinguished at the last but not by boys on scaffolds, not by the likes of young Thorncraft.

GLEANINGS 1819–1832

15 February 1819
On Friday last the following persons were convicted by the Uckfield Bench for offences under the Excise Laws.

Edward Kenward, of Isfield, labourer, in the penalty of £100, for having two quarts of contraband spirits in his possessions.

John Holford, of Framfield, labourer, in the penalty of £50 for selling contraband spirits.

Joseph Seymour, of Buxted, labourer, in the penalty of £50 for having one quart of contraband spirit in his possession.

George Moon, of Waldron, labourer, in the penalty of £100 for having two quarts of contraband spirit in his possession.

The Times 13 August 1819
Corporal James M'Cabe said that he came immediately to the spot after the gun was fired and lifted the deceased up; he died in about 20 minutes. Witness took the prisoner (Edward Broadbent) into custody and on his way to the guard room said to him, 'Are you not a terrible man for doing such a thing as this?' The prisoner replied, 'I am not for the sergeant was always tyrannizing over me and I was determined he should not do it any more.

30 August 1819

On the arrival of the cart under the fatal tree, the Rev. Mr. Noyce, the clergyman in attendance, ascended it and began to pray, requesting the unhappy man to join him; but this, Piper refused to do, saying he was a murdered man. He went on to observe that there was no law for a poor man and referred to a case at our last Assizes wherein one prisoner was condemned to death and another, charged with a similar crime, was sentenced to two months' imprisonment.

3 April 1820

At our House of Correction on Thursday last, Flagellation was the Order of the Day. The Governor had to superintend six private and two public whippings, which latter punishment attracted the curiosity of several women who, without shame, pressed forward to view the bloody backs of the offenders, Edward Ridley for corn stealing and Thomas Blaber for a misdemeanour.

17 April 1820

Peter Thomas, for stealing one hempen sack, the property of James Foard, of Petworth – One month's solitary confinement.

John Berryman and John Goble, convicted of stealing three fowls and one turkey in the parish of Sutton and William Chantler, convicted of stealing 14 live fowls, the property of Ann Kempshall, of Horsham, were severally sentenced to Seven Years Transportation.

25 September 1820

Frederick Reader, of notorious memory, though only fifteen years of age, has again been examined by our Bench of Magistrates, on a charge of robbery; but again, in default of evidence, discharged. His similarly aged and equally depraved associates, Skirlock and Bonner, together with a fourth named Jenkins, were more implicated in the charge than Reader, but these evade detection. As nothing but transportation or the gallows it seems can put a stop to their infamous career, young as they are, for nothing in the shape of advice or a pointing out of consequences, is regarded by them, we may conclude that it will not be long ere we have again to report progress to their disadvantage.

The Times 22 December 1830

The prisoner (Edward Bushby of East Preston) was immediately called up for judgment and the learned Judge having assumed the black cap, told the prisoner that he had been found guilty upon clear and satisfactory evidence of a crime punishable by the laws of this country with death. The sentence of death was not always carried into full effect; but the offence of arson was of that description, and particularly at the present time was one of so alarming a character, that if not checked, the country would be plunged into ruin and desolation. 'I dare not,' added the learned Judge, 'consistently with my duty to the public, recommend you to His Majesty as an object of mercy.'

An Authentic and Faithful History of the Atrocious Murder of Celia Holloway by John Holloway, Brighton's first trunk murderer. 1831

I asked her to sit down on the stairs and then on the pretence of kissing her, I passed a line around her neck and strangled her. When I thought she was dead or nearly dead, I dragged her into a cupboard under the stairs. I cut off her head first.

27 February 1832

At 3 a.m. in broad moonlight, a boat containing about 300 tubs of spirits was beached opposite Stafford's library and a party of 200 men succeeded in clearing nearly all the tubs with which they proceeded along the Steyne and up the (Worthing) High Street, guarded by a company of Bexhill batmen with a few firearms and closely followed by a small party of Prevention men.

At the top of High Street, Lieutenant Henderson and four of his men met and immediately pressed upon the smugglers who made their way over into the Brooks; and here the parties had a skirmish; one of the Prevention men was knocked down and another had his breastbone broken by a stone.

The smugglers, with a man of the name of Cowardson as their leader, formed line and came with many oaths upon Lieutenant Henderson who, maintaining the greatest coolness, warned them not to come near him and threatened to shoot the first man that advanced; but they still closed on him, when Cowardson, with his bat raised, being in the act of striking, Lieutenant Henderson shot him dead upon the spot and with his second pistol wounded another man in the thigh.

The above extracts are from the *Sussex Weekly Advertiser*, except where stated.

7

HARD TIMES

JANE GOLDSMITH just happened to look in William Heasman's garden as she was passing. Looked quite casually at the pig pen. Weighed up his winter vegetable patch. Glanced at his chickens. . . and it was then that she saw the pullet and had no doubt about it, none at all. Back she went to her master, Thomas Foster. She had seen the pullet, she told him.

Straightaway Foster, trusting his housekeeper's word, sent for his son, Isaac, schoolmaster and unpaid constable of the Hundred of Barcombe, Hamsey and Newick.

That pullet, he said, the one that had been stolen from his smallholding ten days earlier along with a couple of hens and a young chick. Well, it was in Heasman's garden. You might know, of course, it would be at Heasman's. Shiftless sort of fellow – and although nothing had ever been proved against him, everybody knew what he was like, the sorts of things he got up to.

When Isaac Foster called at Heasman's cottage he refused to believe the man's protestations that the bird belonged to him and that until recently his brother, foreman on another farm some miles away, had been looking after it. The constable had heard such tales before and insisted upon looking around the inside of the cottage.

It was this incident in October 1839 that led to the arrest and trial of a number of Barcombe men. However, although the pullet in Heasman's garden was undeniably stolen, Thomas Foster was mistaken. It was not his bird.

In the lean years of the 1830s petty crime was endemic. Poachers, unde-terred by the severe Game Laws, were out with nets and traps; barns were broken into; hen coops were raided; sacks of corn were stolen. The parish constables, supported fitfully by patrols, sometimes armed, rarely made a capture.

Sheep stealers were as elusive as any of these midnight thieves. They were practised enough at their work, capable of cornering any animal, wrestling it to the ground, despatching it with a knife and then swiftly, in the dark, butchering it crudely on the spot.

On the morning after, some shepherd or farm labourer would come across the sawn off head, the scattered liver and lights, the severed feet, the stripped-off fleece. The carcase would be gone and only occasionally might the searchers find a trail of blood or footmarks in the mud or morning frost. Only rarely did such trails lead anywhere significant.

On the day when Isaac Foster insisted on looking inside Heasman's cottage, however, hoping to find evidence of his father's other missing birds, he did not expect what he found.

There was no sign of the hens or the chick. What the constable found in the kitchen were crocks of salted mutton and suet, a piece of boiled meat and the remains of a mutton pudding. Were these the remains of sheep slain at Flood's Close, Heasman was asked.

He was escorted to Lewes by the constable and here, facing the examining magistrate, Heasman conceded that matters looked bad. He had a wife, four children under ten, a mother. If he were to be transported, and this was certainly likely, he might never see them again. Unless he came to some arrangement. He did so.

Over the next two weeks, Heasman made fourteen statements, confessing to fifteen thefts of sheep. It is certain that the full tally of his offences between 1836 and 1839 was never admitted. But what William Heasman did in turning 'approver' was to implicate several others in his offences so earning his own immunity.

❏ ❏ ❏ ❏ ❏ ❏

In November 1839, the so-called Barcombe Gang of Sheepstealers, comprising half a dozen men from the village, went on trial at Lewes Quarter Sessions. James Towner, 30; William Miles, 21; George Day, 22; Philip Elphick, 24; and Richard Funnell, 45, all farm labourers, pleaded not guilty. John Jenner, 36, a trug maker and carpenter, pleaded guilty to four offences, presumably in the expectation that he would be leniently treated.

From the start it was quite clear that in most of the charges brought Heasman had been the instigator and that he was involved in each of them. This 'smooth faced, light haired, gawky country man' gave evidence against his neighbours 'in a quiet and unconcerned manner, as if he had been the most innocent person in the world, describing the details of each robbery with perfect coolness and without the least hesitation.'

James Towner, who at the time was in regular work, was to blame Heasman for 'always enticing me to do something'. But the mutton found in his house, to which Heasman had alerted the constable, was difficult for a poor man to explain away.

There was no doubt in the constable's mind that this mutton came from the raid at Flood's Close. Towner persevered, however, painting Heasman as a constant tempter, a man who had scorned him for being under the thumb of a wife who refused to allow him to go out seeking sheep.

'I never see what a damned wife you have got, Towner,' Heasman had told him. 'She'll never let you go anywhere along with me.'

He had threatened Towner that if he knew of anyone saying anything against him or trying to hurt him, 'he would hurt them in any kind of way by poisoning their Hog if they had one or destroy their Bees for he would have his revenge.'

John Jenner spoke of Heasman's power and influence too. 'He was the ringleader and has been for years in Barcombe,' he said. 'Heasman drawed me into these things.'

The Earl of Chichester, presiding, and the jury heard each of the men in turn describe how the principal prosecution witness had been the one to lead them on. Philip Elphick suggested that he would never accompany Heasman, although he had been invited to do so. 'My mother and father would be crazy if ever I did,' he told the court.

Richard Funnell, the oldest of the accused, denied that he had been out with Heasman several times. It was not that he had not been asked, either. 'He often wanted me to but I never would,' he said.

No, he said, he had not been over to Knowland Farm and taken two sheep. Nor had he been to John Rickman's farm at Wellingham. Nor at Cowleaze Farm either. And he denied killing and flaying one of Henry Kell's animals in a field and hiding the carcase in a barn where during the day he was threshing.

Heasman had explained how over the next few days both men had taken home cuts of lamb, just as they needed them, smuggling them away under their smocks, but Funnell strenuously denied this account.

Despite Heasman's accusations – which were probably true – Funnell was acquitted. As there was no evidence other than that of Heasman, the prosecution withdrew the case. Further corroborative testimony was essential, said the Earl of Chichester, presumably feeling some distaste for the part the chief witness was playing.

Chichester had no doubt about Funnell's guilt, however, dismissing him with the hope that 'he would avoid such practices in future and shun the bad company in which he had evidently been.'

Jenner had no inhibitions about admitting his guilt. 'That's all right – I am guilty of that concern,' he said about a theft of four sheep. 'I had got work at that time and Heasman had none. He came to me and said he was starving and said if you don't like to go with me, I must get another mate.'

One night the two men had gone on a foray markedly different from any other in which they had engaged. They broke into the dairy at Cowleaze Farm.

The theft was discovered at 5.30am by Jane Bristow, one of the servants who had gone to the dairy at that early hour to get milk for the farm workers' breakfast. She found missing 'one large crock of butter, two large hams, two hands and two cheeks of pork, one eye piece, four knuckles, four pig's feet and about six pounds of pickled pork. . . the hog had been killed about a month before.'

The two thieves had gone home, each with his share. The butter, however, was put in the river and retrieved the following night. This was one of the offences that Jenner had admitted.

William 'Squat' Miles was accused of having helped Heasman steal sixteen chickens from a farm but he denied this and the charge was withdrawn. He also denied that one night, being out of work and desperate, he had gone to Heasman. They had discussed what to do – at least, Heasman said they had, for Miles denied the whole tale – and they had decided to 'get a little Wheat and have it ground into flour'. They agreed, so the story went, to meet later that night and Miles went back to bed in the cottage where he lodged.

'I was to pull a string on his finger,' Heasman explained. ' I went according to agreement at 12 o'clock and called him and he came down.'

The following day, when the theft of a bag of wheat from Clayhill Farm was discovered, the tracks of the two men were followed by the bailiff and a carter along the winter pathways. The parish constable, a shoemaker by trade, thought one of the footprints was distinctive and consulted another Barcombe shoemaker who recognised the sole of Miles' boot which he had recently repaired. At the time the evidence had not been strong enough to bring to court. Now, however, Heasman was confirming it.

Towner, for his part, tried desperately to convince the jury of his innocence. It was Heasman who had called on him one night at 11 o'clock. Towner's wife had pulled him back into bed, refusing to let him go sheep stealing. Four or five hours later, when Heasman had returned with some cuts of lamb, wanting to hide them in Towner's lodge, ' I told him it was not a fitting place and that he should not put it in'.

No, Towner said, he had never gone on one of Heasman's nocturnal expeditions. But the mutton found in his house the day Heasman was arrested? What about that? What about the suet, too? And the greasy sack?

Towner had told the magistrate how, when in work, he had bought meat when he could.

'I have had a breast of mutton nearly every week. Sometimes a pound and a half of suet, sometimes two pounds, sometimes half a pound, sometimes the Bones,' his statement reads. 'And the Bones I have broke and stewed them and made Broth.'

As for the suet, he had had it 'done up to make cakes for the children which was cheaper than Bread and Cheese and Meat'.

Poor Towner, a loving family man, told how one day he had resisted one of Heasman's proposals. 'I had one of my children in my arms,' he said. This was the man who, when arrested, spoke to Isaac Foster, the constable, 'with feeling of his children'.

But in court Heasman told them how 'as I was going up Barcombe Lane after a pail of water, James Towner followed me'. It was then, according to Heasman, that Towner asked, 'What do you say about going after a sheep tonight? I want one unaccountably.'

In court the accusations, claims and counter claims went on over two days. All but those against Miles, Jenner and Towner were dismissed.

One charge only was proceeded against in the case of Miles, that of the theft of a sack of wheat at Clayhill Farm. Finding him guilty, the jury 'recommended the prisoner to the mercy of the Court, in consequence of his having been drawn into the commission of the crime by an older man.'

He was sentenced to one year's hard labour to include four separate fortnights of solitary confinement.

James Towner faced only one charge – the theft of three sheep from Flood's Close. He was found guilty and sentenced to ten years' transportation.

John Jenner was found guilty on four charges. As he had pleaded guilty to three of them he might have expected some generosity of treatment and his sentence for these was four days' imprisonment. He admitted a fifth charge of breaking into the dairy at Cowleaze Farm and for that he was sentenced to fifteen years' transportation.

The rest of the accused returned to their homes, to their intermittent employment, to their unremitting poverty. Is it possible that they were guilty of what they were charged with? Were Heasman's accusations well founded? Very likely.

Miles was later transported for the theft of some clothing. Towner served his sentence and returned to Barcombe after a few years. Jenner's wife in the 1841 Census is described as a pauper and a widow.

And Heasman, whose theft of a pullet was to lead to the trial of half a dozen of his neighbours, left the district and has not been traced.

The Barcombe Gang of Sheep Stealers is how they are described in the *Brighton Gazette* in November 1839. But was it really a gang?

Come to that, were they really criminals? Or was the worst crime which Heasman committed the betrayal of the men of his village?

Finally there is a powerful and lasting image of a Barcombe woman, the wife of one of the sheep stealers who was sentenced to be transported in 1838. She had walked to Portsmouth from her village near Lewes.

Now she stands on the harbour wall. The tide turns and the boat leaves harbour taking her husband on his long, desperate journey to the other side of the world.

She waves and waves but there is no response from on board. She remains on the wall, still waving, until finally the boat is lost to sight.

GLEANINGS 1835 1838

William Ford's handwritten deposition,
signed with his mark
11 February 1835

I keep The Royal Oak Public House in Longbridge in the Parish of Lullington in this County. Yesterday evening the Prisoners Richard Lower and Stephen Lewis came into my House and called for a Pint of Beer. They afterwards had two Pints more and remained in the House till about quarter past nine. I had some Bacon Hams in my Kitchen Chimney. In the course of the day as I sat by the fire I noticed that the Hams were in the Chimney two or three times. There were three Hams there at those times. I noticed that the prisoner Lower appeared to be watching me about the House which made me suspicious of him. The other prisoner Stephen Lewis gave me a little Pook [poke] and pointed up the Chimney. I called my wife to wait in the Kitchen and went out at the Back Door and sent my next door Neighbour Mrs. Burfield for Edward Reeds who lives close by. I returned immediately to the Kitchen and the Prisoner went out of the House almost directly. I then looked up the Chimney with a Candle. I discovered that one Ham of the three was gone. I asked my daughter who had come in from the Bar into the Kitchen whether she had taken one of the Hams down. She said No. I am not certain whether I asked my wife the same question or whether she was in the Kitchen or at the Bar Door when I asked my daughter. I then went out of doors and I saw the Prisoner come back into the House. I went up to the Prisoner Lower and asked him what he had done with the Ham. He said he did not know anything about it. I told him I was certain he did know. He said if I would let him go he would tell me where it was. I told him I should not let him go till somebody else came. He said he would go and fetch it. I told him he should go in a-doors and I led him in a-doors. He still wanted to go after the Bacon but I told him I would not let him go till somebody else came. James Cox a neighbour soon came in. I asked Cox to take the Man to go with him after the Bacon. In three or four Minutes they came back with Edward Reeds who had the Bacon in his Hand. I saw the Ham and was sure it was my Ham. All that Lower said and did was quite voluntary. I sent for the Constable, Richard Hilton, and delivered the Prisoner to him.

18 February 1837

The Constable proceeded to Fowler's cottage in Pevensey and just as he entered it the inmates were preparing to dine off a sheep's head: this was a strong confirmation of the justness of the suspicions entertained, and it was immediately afterwards fully confirmed, for on prosecuting the search, the remainder of the animal was found salted down.

25 February 1837

George Head, 14, labourer, was charged with having stolen nine worsted cravats, value 4s. at Brighton, the property of Joseph Dowling. A previous conviction of felony, on the 10th October, 1836, was then put in and read. Transported for seven years.

18 March 1837

William Phillips, baker, 29, charged with feloniously killing at Brighton, George Thomas Daniel. Owing to the absence of three principal witnesses, the case was stayed, and under the direction of his Lordship the prisoner was acquitted.

25 March 1837

On the evening of yesterday se'nnight, about half past eight o'clock, as Mr. James Whitfield's carter was on return to his master's farm at Falmer, he was stopped on the highway by three men and two women. He was pinioned by the shoulders and arms while one of the female depredators robbed him of a yellow canvas bag containing in gold, silver and copper, £3 1s. 6d., the remaining change of a £5 note, with which he had been entrusted to pay his master's workmen. The miscreants got clear off. When will this disgraceful state of things be put an end to by the authorities? Depredations are now so frequent on this road that it is now palpably unsafe to travel alone and unarmed.

13 May 1837

EAST HOATHLY – a few nights since some thieves carried off from the farm of Mr. Marten, the leaden pump and piping. This they accomplished without creating alarm there being no residence at hand. Lead stealing has of late increased and several felons are now in the Lewes Gaol, awaiting their trials for offences of this kind.

3 June 1837

BRIGHTON – Last Saturday morning, about two o'clock, a baker named Gregory, was aroused from his slumbers by his wife who heard a noise downstairs. Gregory immediately went downstairs with a pistol in his hand, where he found two men who had affected an entrance through the bakehouse, and had collected together considerable booty. The pistol was not loaded and the baker in his hurry presented the butt end of it and courageously exclaimed, 'If you stir, I'll shoot you.' Fortunately the cover of night befriended the baker and the burglars, inasmuch as they did not discover his mistake, being alarmed at his sudden appearance, begged for mercy. His wife in the meantime had alarmed the neighbourhood and two policemen coming up, they were given into their custody and safely placed in 'durance vile'.

16 September 1837

Philadelphia Martin, aged 37, (on bail) was indicted with fraudulently obtaining by means of false pretences, on the 28th July last, at Ticehurst, four pounds of mutton, the property of John Standen and Thomas Standen and on the 28th August last, eight pounds weight of mutton and one pound weight of suet, the property of John Standen and Thomas Standen. The prisoner pleaded guilty. The witness gave her a good character for former conduct and said that she has a family of eight children, seven of whom are under twelve years of age. The court sentenced her to be imprisoned for the first offence for one week and for the second a fortnight in solitary confinement.

20 January 1838

On Tuesday morning last, George Baker of New Town, on his release from Petworth House of Correction for poaching was immediately delivered into the custody of Toler who was in waiting, and replaced in the House under a warrant; he, Baker, not having appeared at the Sessions to answer a charge by Mr. William Hill of Sompting, for stealing two pigs a long time since.

Except where stated, the above extracts are from the
Sussex Agricultural Express

8

A CASTE APART

22 October 1850 *The Times*
There is a criminal population dispersed throughout the length and breadth of the land -- a caste apart which daily and hourly recruits its ranks from all that is most idle, dissolute and unprincipled among us. The hands of this Bedouin horde are against every man.

HARRIET STONER woke suddenly. Something had roused her. She listened for a while then climbed out of bed and went to the window. It was very early but the summer sky was already lightening. She heard the noise again. A creaking at the foot of the stairs. She went across to the bedroom door, opened it, and called out for Edward. But no Edward called back. There was a light below in the shop. She could see it through a crack in the door at the bottom of the stairs. Thank God, it was bolted.

More noise

'What are you after there?' she called, hoping it might be Edward about his duties,

The door burst open, flung off its hooks, and two men with pistols were bounding up the stairs. She was seized and thrown down in a corner of the passage. They crowded over her, holding her down. 'The money', they shouted. 'Come on, come on! If you don't tell us, we'll blow your brains out'

She feels the muzzles of the horse pistols against her forehead. A third man is flourishing a chisel across her face and throat. They ask her about the money again and again

'Blow her brains out if she doesn't tell.'

How can she tell? One of them has his hand over her nose and mouth, another grasps her by the throat.

Months later Mrs Stoner was to tell the court: 'I was very much alarmed. My breath was nearly gone and I was almost fainting.' She remembered someone, possibly a fourth man, coming into the passage. He had found her keys in the bedroom.

'Take them and find your money,' she was ordered.'We are come for your money and we will have it or your life.'

'Spare my life,' she begged the men. 'Lord have mercy upon me.'

She was dragged by the hair back into her bedroom where the robbers found £7 10s in gold and between £3 and £4 in silver in the room.

Although shaken, Mrs Stoner followed them out of the front door and saw Edward Enticknap, the shopman, at the mercy of another armed man and being threatened exactly as she had been. Edward, realising what was happening, had bided his time, had done nothing rash, had tiptoed down a back staircase from his room and once out of the house had called out: 'Murder', before being pulled up by one of the robbers. Now he stood, almost naked, just as he had come from his bed, with a pistol pointed at him.

Then abruptly, all of the men left.

Mrs Stoner and Edward found everything in confusion in the grocery shop. The shutter of the back window had been destroyed and the window smashed. In the shop they found a dark lantern. Upstairs there was a chisel and a man's cap. A brass candlestick was missing and some spoons, one of them silver.

After leaving the house, the robbers made their way to a wood a couple of miles further on, near Plaistow. Here the takings were shared out – three shillings and sixpence per man. They could have made that amount with less risk from a couple of days' labouring.

But 3s 6d? Was that all? Had not £7 10s in gold been taken and £3 or £4 in silver? Perhaps not everyone knew precisely how much had been taken. Perhaps some thought that only £1 or so in small coins was all that they had managed to come away with.

For this was a gang in which the members even robbed each other.

This is the first reported attack by the gang. It took place at Kirdford near Petworth in the early hours of 4 June, 1850. Similar attacks, violent and frightening, were repeated at other locations in the course of the next six months.

The leader of the gang was John Isaacs, the man with the chisel. His accomplices were the pistol-carrying Harwood cousins, Levi and Samuel, and James Jones.They were the so-called Guildford men. Other gang members on this raid were John Smith and James Hamilton.

In the summer of 1850 the gang also included John Isaacs' brother, Edward; William Brooks; Thomas Morgan alias Toot; brothers John and James Smith; Joseph Carter; William Hillyer; and Richard Trowler alias Hiram Smith. They were, in the main, in their twenties and thirties.

On the periphery of the gang was Elizabeth Oliver, who lived with

Brooks, and who was often responsible for the concealment and the onward movement of stolen goods. Others involved were Brooks' uncle and aunt, James and Sarah Edwards, who had a cottage on Crowborough Common stacked with stolen articles awaiting purchasers and Elizabeth Howis, Brooks' sister and James Gulliver.

Hamilton was to describe in court how the gang was organised. 'John Isaacs was duly elected captain,' he said, 'and we were all sworn to obey his orders; and if anyone attempted to back out or refused to take part in any robbery or murder, if necessary he or she was to be instantly shot, and if anyone left the gang without the consent of the captain, he or she was to be followed, and if overtaken, to be shot.'

The Guildford men chose to live in low taverns and beer shops. Others, such as Hillyer, Carter and Morgan, lived in heathland huts and tents.

How did they appear to those they menaced? Just occasionally individuals among them are lit up by a stray sentence or the odd graphic paragraph. At their trial three of them were described by *The Times* reporter:.

'Hiram Smith is about the middle height with narrow contracted shoulders and a stooping figure. His face is extremely forbidding in expression, the features having that sharp prominent character which marks the rogue while the doubtful and hesitating glance of the eye indicates a disposition at once cunning and irresolute.'

Only four years older than Hiram Smith, Levi Harwood at twenty-nine was an even more fearsome looking character.

'Levi Harwood is a ruffianly looking man, square built and evidently possessing considerable physical strength. His features are coarse and rugged and his face betrays the mastery of violent passions. He looks like one of those idle fellows, half-hostlers, half anything else, who are seen loitering about country inns and waiting for any job that may turn up for them.'

And the third member?

'James Jones is also about the middle size, his features flat and repulsive and his whole physiognomy expressive of a life of depravity and crime. Both he and Levi Harwood look like bold determined fellows, capable of carrying through any deed of violence they may once have undertaken.'

These were men who led brutal lives. They were a shiftless crew, a gallery of rogues, of reckless character, each seeming to match his neighbour in viciousness. They seemed to have little fear, less shame.

Let it be remembered that Kirdford was not the first crime the gang committed. It is simply the first burglary of which there is any known detail.

Shortly after Kirdford, in July 1850, Brooks, Hamilton and the two Isaacs were encamped on Copthorne Common. Brooks, also a hawker, had planned a raid at Haywards Heath on the house of two elderly spinsters, the Misses Kennard. After their briefing, the gang members travelled separately to their target.

When the gang arrived at the house located on the common, not far from Haywards Heath station, there was a ladder in the garden which they used to climb up to the window of a room in which there was a light. A female servant was sleeping there on a temporary bed, looking after a sick manservant.

It is difficult to understand why the safest and usual mode of entry – by the ground floor – was not adhered to. And why choose a room showing a light? Obviously it was occupied and the occupant might have been awake. Although professional thieves could make an entry through a window quite quickly, there was no guarantee that someone in a room would not just have time to raise the alarm.

Were the robbers sure that no one would raise the alarm at the Misses Kennard's house? Had the servant in the bedroom been primed by one of the gang? Was the ladder deliberately placed in the garden? After all, servants were not uniformly honest.

After entering the room, the men broke down the Misses Kennard's bedroom door, threatening to blow out the women's brains if they tried to raise the alarm. Then they set about their work.

At the end of a two-hour session, during which time they visited the pantry to eat and drink, they left with a considerable haul.

Isaacs went to London to fence the stolen goods but claimed on his return to have sold only one gold coin. Each man received thirty shillings. What other excuses Isaacs offered are not recorded although it appears that there was a quarrel when the others heard that he had bought a new wagon.

It was at this stage that Richard Trowler, alias Hiram Smith, made his appearance. At twenty-five years of age, he had 'the slight, active figure of the accomplished burglar with a cast of countenance at once cunning, cowardly and cruel'.

He was a pot boy in a pub at the age of eighteen and had taken up with a band of tramping hawkers – those rural nomads, mouchers and cadgers, not quite the traditional vagrants but men who might do occasional odd jobs and commit occasional crimes. He was the son of a transportee and a footloose, unreliable sort of man. He was an admitted burglar who had been arrested on suspicion of other crimes.

Smith had known Levi Harwood for three years when they, along with an unidentified third man, broke into the vicarage at Upper Dicker on 20 September, 1850. The three masked men entered the main house via the wash house window and went first to the servants' bedroom where they helped themselves to 'two common watches'. Next they went into the vicar's bedroom.

The Reverend Mr Owen Vidal, a man in his early thirties and a future Bishop of Sierra Leone, woke to find a masked man in a dark coat standing over him. In one hand the intruder held a tallow candle and in the other a sword. A shorter man carrying an axe handle came into the room. Where was the money, he wanted to know.

Vidal was dragged to his study and the desk drawers were opened. Silver and gold were taken. At one point, the clergyman 'earnestly remonstrated with the ruffian (the one armed with the sword) reminding him of the fate which must await him before a God of justice hereafter even if he escaped punishment in this world.'

In response the sword was drawn across the vicar's throat. Any noise and it would be used on him.

In another room, Miss Capper, the housekeeper, managed to hide a gold watch. When her valuables were demanded she offered her Bible. If Mr Vidal could offer the thieves sermons, then his housekeeper could present them with a potent symbol. The robbers, unsurprisingly, were not deterred.

Despite Mr Vidal's offer of a reward of £20 and despite its later being raised by the Home Office to £50, no one was charged with this offence.

□ □ □ □ □

The murder at Frimley in Surrey was to deal a major blow to the activities of the Isaacs gang. It took four of them – Hiram Smith, James Jones and the Harwoods – permanently out of circulation.

It was a robbery that went wrong. A clergyman was shot in his bedroom and the men escaped in panic.

Within days they were all under arrest. Inspector Hollington of the Guildford police heard of the murder and burglary, made inquiries, and discovered that on the night of the murder they were all missing from their lodgings. Of all the criminals in the area, these were the men the meagre

Levi Harwood and James Jones were hanged before a crowd of 7,000 spectators at Horsemonger Lane Goal, Southwark.

ranks of the police instantly suspected.

It was Hiram Smith's evidence for the prosecution that led to the hanging of two of his companions, Levi Harwood and James Jones. Smith was only too anxious to offer evidence on behalf of the Crown if it guaranteed his safety.

Thus, by September 1850, a significant element of the Isaacs gang was removed. In another three months or so, the gang was completely broken up.

Smith was, incidentally, suspected of the murder of George Griffith at Newtimber in 1849. It has been suggested that he would have been charged with the crime in 1850 had he not offered to 'approve' in the Frimley case.

There was a lull in activity after the arrest of those involved in the affair at Frimley. By November, however, the gang committed another violent robbery at Frensham Common.

Some days later tools were taken from Mr Knight's workshop at Maresfield. The gang was equipping itself for more housebreaking. In mid December, the Six Bells at Chailey was broken into.

Isaacs did not take part in any of the autumn or early winter break ins.

By Christmas, however, he was ready with more plans. He travelled from Reading by train and was met by Hamilton at Woking Station. They made their way to Edenbridge, meeting the others – the two Smiths, Morgan, Hillyer, Brooks and Elizabeth Oliver with her baby – in a barn on 31 December, 1850.

Isaacs presented the group with two targets. The major break-in was to be at Uckfield but he proposed a local robbery that very evening. While some of the party – Hamilton, Brooks and James Smith – went on towards Crowborough, the remainder, led by Isaacs, went to Old Pie Corner, Hartfield, and burgled the White Hart.

The next morning, 1 January 1851, the two groups met up in Crowborough Forest where they shared plum cake, wine and tobacco, all by courtesy of the White Hart, which had also lost a bundle of calico and some silver spoons.

They now prepared for the robbery at Downland House, a mansion occupied by three elderly sisters, the Misses Farncombe. In the evening, Isaacs, Hamilton and Carter arrived in Uckfield and waited outside the house until the lights went out. Later the others joined them.

At two or three o'clock, they forced entry through the dairy window and got into the kitchen. Here they found some clothes which provided them with a temporary disguise. Carter and Brooks put on women's bonnets and the others pulled on coats belonging to the butler, Thomas Wood.

Elsewhere in the house, a maid, Frances Carey, alarmed at the noise downstairs, opened a window and rang her handbell. Mary Farncombe screamed from her single bedroom and her sister Elizabeth, ignoring the burglars, went across the passage to her room.

Wood, the butler, was bustled by the robbers downstairs to the pantry. The men were nervous, he said, some of them anxious to leave, others determined to finish the job and all hastily throwing food and silver plate into an apron.

Eventually, the gang left with property estimated at £300. It was a successful haul.

It was also the last jaunt of John Isaacs' gang.

Returning to Crowborough the men stopped in a wood for a substantial breakfast of hare, veal, roast mutton, ham, pork, bread and cheese, after which they settled down to divide the money.

'We all shared this after breakfast,' Hamiltonwas to tell the court, 'a sovereign and 7s. each but there was a deal more money smuggled among themselves.'

Then he gave a revealing account of how criminal gangs determined the always knotty problem of sharing their loot.

'After the breakfast and after the sharing of the money we looked the plate over and broke up what we thought was not silver. There were two gold watches and two silver ones. The two gold watches were along with the plate, and the silver plate which came from the Old Pie public house was put along with it. The two silver watches were put up amongst us for those who would give most for them. Carter was the highest bidder at 11s for the small watches; and the other one, a double-cased one, was taken by Morgan for 25s. Isaacs took all the plate etc in a flag basket. . .Hillyer took the cutlass.'

At this point, the party divided, agreeing to meet some days later at Warlingham. Isaacs went off towards London and the others to their various destinations. Hamilton and the Smith brothers made for the Rose and Crown at Groombridge, just over the county border into Kent, where they spent the afternoon and evening drinking.

They were clearly drunk when a quarrel broke out between John Smith and Hamilton. The latter dropped a sovereign and Smith picked it up, proffering a shilling in its stead. Befuddled though he was, Hamilton knew the difference between a sovereign and a shilling.

Hamilton said that in the ensuing argument he feared the brothers were going to set about him so he demanded the local constable be sent for.

Quite absurd.

The consequence was that John Smith was taken in charge and led off to Tunbridge Wells. He seems to have submitted quietly.

Quite remarkable.

Hamilton stayed the night in a bedroom at the Rose and Crown and James Smith, the seventeen year old, bedded down in the stables. Prior to retiring Hamilton had handed over 18s 6d to the landlady for safekeeping. He was undoubtedly the most experienced thief on the premises but he clearly placed little trust in his fellows.

When Hamilton went to retrieve his money the next morning, the landlady refused to hand it over until she had spoken to the constable. The grounds for her stance are not clear. Perhaps she had thought over his behaviour of the previous day and had become more suspicious of him. The constable was summoned again but uncertain what to do, did nothing. Hamilton and Smith, deciding to cut their losses, set off on the road to Tunbridge Wells.

The previous day the three men had left some of their haul in a wood and now Hamilton and Smith went to find it. Shortly afterwards a posse of half a dozen men overtook them and with obviously stolen property in their possession – a £5 note on the Lewes Bank, an umbrella, a steel tobacco box and a lucifer box – they were placed under arrest. The two thieves were taken to Tunbridge Wells.

Superintendent Morton of Tunbridge Wells questioned Hamilton about about the items in his possession including a piece of black cotton, his mask, found in his pocket.

'He said, "I have had it a long time; I had it to take bees,"' said the officer. 'I searched him further and found this black checked coat under his over one. I inquired of him how he became possessed of that coat.

"I bought it off a Jew in London after the last hopping."

'I afterwards searched James Smith. I found in one of his pockets the pink handkerchief. (Identified as belonging to one of the Farncombe sisters.)

'I said: Where did you get this from?

'He answered, "I found it a month ago."

'I asked Hamilton where he got the apron which he was seen wearing.

'He replied: "My uncle gave it to me about three days ago. His name is Wilson and he lives in Brighton."

'I inquired of him where he got the £5 note on the Lewes Bank.

'He said: "I sold a pony some time back at Farnham Fair and that is the money I received."

'I afterwards asked him how he became possessed of the umbrella and he observed that he had one the night before but it was stolen from the public house.'

But soon Hamilton lost confidence in his story. He knew that the evidence was stacked up against him. He would be 'boated' way across to the other side of the world.

Unless, of course, he turned Queen's Evidence.

Hillyer and Morgan were arrested at The Swan in Guildford. Carter, at Woking Common, was disarmed and arrested.

Elizabeth Oliver was picked up in a crowd outside Tunbridge Wells Police Station. She was watching the prisoners being taken in and was recognised as an accomplice. She was searched by Superintendent Morton's wife who found sovereigns, watches and jewellery hidden in her underskirts. One of the watches had been subjected to 'a process called "christening", that is the plate had been turned upside down and the name and number obliterated.'

Some weeks later John Isaacs was apprehended at Frome in the process of planning other robberies.

In January, Superintendent Dodson of Tunbridge Wells 'scoured Surrey, Sussex, Berkshire, Hampshire, Wiltshire and Oxfordshire' searching for Brooks, finally running him to ground in the Woking area.

In the cottage at Crowborough occupied by Brooks' aunt and uncle, the police found a 'quantity of the most heterogeneous description. . . jackets, trousers, shawls, silk and cotton handkerchiefs, calicoes, pillowcases'. Cartloads of stolen goods were recovered by the police.

On the way from Tunbridge Wells to trial at Lewes, because the offences with which they were charged had been committed in Sussex, the party of manacled prisoners led by Brooks tried to escape from the open cart in which they were being carried but failed.

Isaacs later attempted an escape from Lewes gaol and all but succeeded in getting away.

At the Assizes at Lewes, Hamilton's evidence convicted six of the men who burgled the Misses Farncombe's house at Uckfield. These were Brooks, the two Smiths, Morgan, Hillyer and Carter. Edward Isaacs was found guilty of burglary at Haywards Heath. These seven were transported for life.

James Gulliver, Elizabeth Howis and Elizabeth Oliver, 'a respectable looking young countrywoman', with her baby in her arms, were found guilty of receiving and transported for fourteen years.

John Isaacs and Samuel Harwood, found guilty of the robbery at Kirdford, were also transported for life.

Brooks' uncle, James Edwards, who had kept a veritable store house of stolen goods on Crowborough Common, was given a modest two years' imprisonment after his employer, a builder, gave him a good character reference.

James Hamilton who claimed to be 'in considerable peril' was kept in police custody, until 'his services can be dispensed with'. The last sight of him comes from the *Brighton Guardian* as he contemplates the same destination as most of his former companions.

'The man Hamilton is enjoying the sea breezes under the surveillance of the Brighton Police, waiting for a free passage to Australia which has been promised to him.'

And Hiram Smith, whose testimony had consigned Levi Harwood and James Jones to the scaffold, what of him? He appeared at the Surrey Summer Assizes and was discharged. There is no indication of where his future led him.

How then is the Isaacs gang which caused such havoc and distress to be assessed? As thieves, how successful were they?

For the most part, their targeting was sound. They tended to select lone houses with occupants they considered easy victims such as elderly ladies and in two cases, clergymen.

The gang escaped with some significant hauls. It was estimated that in the course of two years they netted goods and money to the value of £1,500. Today's valuation might be at least a hundred times greater.

Their planning too was generally good. They could be assembled, dismissed in pairs or individuals and reformed in new locations very quickly. They marched to their various destinations by night, picking their way across wastes and heathland or even on one occasion along the railway line.

But successful?

It seems not. In financial terms, despite the rich hauls, they always seemed hard-up. When arrested, Hamilton was penniless. Hiram Smith had his belongings in the pawn shop and the others seemed anxious to steal the smallest amounts from their companions.

Perhaps Isaacs was the only one to do well out of the business. He had bought a new wagon. But that they were representative of 'the dangerous classes' there is no doubt.

They were violent, reckless men.

They were a caste apart.

GLEANINGS 1839-1850

28 January 1839

WADHURST – The disgraceful riots which so frequently occur at beer shops and ale houses in our parish will now, it is hoped, soon be put a stop to. Warrants are issued against James Sivyer, commonly called Turk, Richard Darnell, a sweep, and Frederick Lee, the principal ring leaders concerned in a riot at Wadhurst Fair on the 1st November last.

29 April 1839

The Royal Commission on Police was informed that Brighton contained numerous lodging houses, the keepers of which furnish matches, songs, laces, and many other petty articles which are hawked about as an excuse of vagrancy and it gives them opportunities of greater consequence, observing the fastenings and other circumstances that may lead to robbery. The principal robberies have been concocted in vagrant lodging houses and rendered effectual through the agencies of the Keepers. Intelligence is given and received by clients.

25 January 1840

William Hunt was charged with having, early on the morning of the 1st inst., shot one hen pheasant in Ponfield in the parish of Northchapel. Committed to Petworth House of Correction for three calendar months to hard labour.

15 April 1840 Brighton Guardian

Stunt said that on the night of the 18th November last, himself, John Wood and Marchant went to Hawkhurst to the house of Mr. Lavender where they took out a square of glass, unfastened the window, and got in. They took a great many articles, and amongst them a desk, a gun, a cloak, and about 12oz. of silver. They brought them all to Jack Wood's and in a few days they started with them for Brighton. Wood carried the gun and offered it for sale as he went along at a blacksmith's shop on Meckham [Magham] Down. They then went on to Brighton and pawned it. The silver was sold and Wood said it went to London that night.

23 May 1840

Thomas Vidler was charged with stealing at Burwash on 9th May, twenty pieces of hop pole, value 3d, belonging to Edward Maynard. He pleaded guilty and said that he picked up the wood to burn. One week's imprisonment in solitary confinement.

George Briggs, 16, labourer, was charged with stealing at the parish of Woolavington on the 18th of February last, two rabbit traps, chains and grapples, value 4s, the property of Cresswell Andrews and two other rabbit traps, chains and grapples, value 4s, the property of Richard Bingham Newland, Esq. Guilty – Ten days' imprisonment to hard labour and once privately whipped.

Michael Torbutt, 27, millwright, was charged with stealing at Ifield, on the 27th of May, one calico shirt, one pair of stockings, and one cotton handkerchief, the property of John Luther Jupp – Guilty. A former conviction of felony being proved, the prisoner was sentenced to ten years' transportation.

William Middleton, 15, sweep, was indited for breaking and entering the dwelling house of George Chalk at the parish of St. Peter the Great, otherwise Subdeanery, on the 10th of June, and stealing therein two silk handkerchiefs, one twopenny piece, 1 metal seal, 1 key, 1 seal, 1 steel chain, a ring and some bread, cheese and bacon, the property of George Chalk. The prisoner was sentenced to be transported for life.

4 July 1840

The report on Lewes House of Correction stated that Hannah McDowell, under sentence of transportation, had petitioned for her discharge on the ground of ill-health; that the petition had been forwarded to the Secretary of State with a recommendation that the prayer of the petition should be granted; that Samuel Byfield, who was sentenced to be transported for life, had been committed to five years' imprisonment upon his petition and had been removed to the Penitentiary; that Richard Thompson, who was sentenced to fourteen years' transportation, prayed for his discharge from custody in consequence of ill-health, the Surgeon's certificate stating that his malady would increase with his imprisonment and advising his petition to be forwarded to the Secretary of State, who had since given him his discharge; that a prisoner named George Primmer, committed on a charge of larceny and who had previously been committed nine times, was found dead in his cell on the 18th of June last, suspended by his neckerchief; and that another prisoner, David Cook, refused to behave properly in (the House of Correction) chapel and had been punished for a breach of the rules, in consequence of which he had been deprived of the privilege of attending chapel.

23 October 1841

For several weeks past an inquiry of the most searching character has been carrying on by the Magistrates of the Lewes Bench and the police, under the direction of Superintendent Fagan, into the circumstances of the death of a woman named Smith, an itinerant dealer in tapes, laces, children's trinkets, etc., who was pursuing her vocation at Ringmer, on the 2nd of June 1838, upwards of three years ago, and was next morning found drowned in a pond near the Rectory. An open verdict of 'Found drowned' being returned, the matter was left open for further investigation. It had long been suspected that there had been some foul play in this mysterious affair, and certain facts having come to the knowledge of the police, a man named General Washer, aged about 60 years, was apprehended on Monday, the 11th inst. on a charge of having murdered the poor woman.

26 March 1842

William Woolven and James Reynolds were brought up for judgment and the former, who had pleaded guilty to four charges of forgery, was ordered to be transported for ten years and the latter was sentence to two years' imprisonment and hard labour.

17 June 1843

A most daring and audacious burglary was committed at the house of Mr. Renville, a farmer at Bolney. It seems that Mr. and Mrs. Renville were alone in the house, having given the man and maid-servant they keep in the house liberty to go to Cowfold club and as they were sitting at supper a person knocked at the door and requested lodging. Mrs. Renville answered the man that they did not receive lodgers when she perceived another standing near, and as soon as Mr. Renville came to the door, they stepped in, followed by four men, the whole six being disguised by wearing crape over their faces. Two of them produced pistols and demanded money and at the same time Mr. Renville, who is an elderly man, was forced into the pantry and locked in, two of the men keeping watch over him. Two of the men stationed themselves at the outside of the house, and the remaining two obliged Mrs. Renville to accompany them upstairs and deliver the money.

HORSE STEALING.
TEN POUNDS REWARD.

WHEREAS, JAMES FUNNELL, is suspected of having stolen, on the 8th of February last, a horse belonging to Mr. William Driver Leadner, of Framfield, in the county of Sussex — Whoever will apprehend, or cause to be apprehended, the said James Funnel, shall receive the said reward of Ten Pounds, upon application to the said Wm. Driver Leadner.

The said James Funnell is about 5 feet 7 or 8 inches high, of a light complexion, light hair, and sandy whiskers, has an impediment in his speech, and is about 27 or 28 years of age. Had on a fustian shooting jacket, corded breeches, and leather boot legs, a rough hat, with a ribbon round it. The woman with whom he cohabits is named Price, whose family is well known in this county.

**John Lawrence's *Last Dying Confession* sold by pedlars
at his execution on 6 April, 1844.
(Lawrence was the last man hanged in Horsham)**

Good people all, I pray draw near,
A dreadful story you shall hear.
Overcome with grief and fear,
I am condemned to die.
I do lament and sore repent
The evil deed which I have done;
My time is come, my glass is run,
I now behold the setting sun,
All in the prime of life.

Chorus
John Lawrence is my name,
To grief and shame
I brought myself this world may see;
Young men a warning take by me,
At Horsham on a fatal tree,
Alas, I am doomed to die.

5 August 1848

Edward Smith was charged with stealing from the person of James Woolcock on the Cup Day of the Races. He was going from the Race Course to Slindon about nine o'clock. Two men came up to him, knocked him down, and took from him a half sovereign and a pocket knife; he had been drinking in a booth all the afternoon and the next day, he went again, and in the same booth he saw a child playing with the identical knife he had been robbed of. He took the knife from the child, fetched a constable, and had the father of the child taken into custody.

The Bench thought there was no case made out and the prisoner was discharged.

£200 REWARD

MURDER

WHEREAS, Mr GEORGE STONEHOUSE GRIFFITH, Brewer, of Brighton, was brutally murdered between Dale Gate and Poynings crossways in the Parish of Newtimber, in the County of Sussex, on Tuesday night, the 6th inst., at 9.30, by some Person or Persons at present unknown, while returning in a Gig from Horsham. The last place he stopped at was the WHITE HART, Henfield, and passed Terry's Cross Gate about Nine o'Clock.

MR GRIFFITH was shot through the Breast with a Pistol or Gun held very near, as his Waistcoat and Shirt were scorched by the fire. He had been 'collecting' and was robbed of a considerable sum of Money, his Book taken, and his Pockets turned inside-out. The Reins were cut, and about a yard of them found under the body. The frame of some Spectacles, covered with black Crape hanging down, and a buck-horn handle Knife with two blades, stamped 'James Green and Co. shear steel, to strike fire,' were left in the road, as also was one of Mr Griffiths Pistols discharged. A Cheque on and crossed to the London and County Bank, Chichester, drawn by John Bower, payable to Henry Bowley, £12 5s. and a £5 note, of the Union Bank, Brighton, torn in two and pasted together, No. D4712, dated June 24th, 1848, and a flat gold Geneva Watch with gold dial, figures painted, black, seconds Hand, with engine turned back, with part of a cable gold Chain attached, were amongst other property stolen from him.

The above Reward of TWO HUNDRED POUNDS will be paid by the undersigned to any Person or Persons who may give such information as shall lead to the apprehension and final conviction of the Murderers.

Information to be given to the Chief Officer of Police, Brighton.
By order of the Police Committee
LEWIS SLIGHT
Clerk to the Commissioners of the
Town of Brighton

7th Feb., 1849

The above extracts are from the *Sussex Agricultural Express* except where otherwise stated.

9

PASSION AND POISON

ALMOST immediately after William French's death some people had doubts. The whispering started almost straightaway. Rumour fed on rumour, busying tongues, so that the events at Gun Hill were gossiped about in every quarter of the parish and beyond.

The thirty one year old farm labourer, they were saying, had died so unexpectedly, and him so healthy. His wife, people said, had been carrying on with another man. A younger man. And her the mother of a little boy, too.

So the tongues certainly wagged.

On 24 December 1851, William French had been at his work, threshing corn in the barn at Stream Farm, Chiddingly. It was back breaking labour that began at seven in the morning and ended at five. French was looking forward to his supper that day. His wife, Sarah, had promised him an onion pie. 'A rarity' was how he described it to his workmate, William Funnell.

However, the next day – Christmas Day – French was ill in bed. The pie, he was to say later, had 'interrupted his insides'.

He remained in bed on Boxing Day and went back to work on Saturday, 27 December, but returned home after only a few minutes. By the Sunday he had recovered and was well enough to go with Sarah to the chapel. The following week he worked without complaint and again on the Sunday went to chapel.

On Monday 5 January, he complained once more of stomach pains and the next two days he had to stay in bed. His wife was saying on the Wednesday that she thought he had improved but late in the evening, just before midnight, he had sat up in bed, turned to her, and muttered his last words:

'You be my wife, bean't you?'

Despite the hour, neighbours came at once and the doctor arrived shortly afterwards. Sarah told him how her husband had suddenly died although she did say that earlier he had been vomiting and had had fainting fits and violent palpitations of the heart. The doctor expressed surprise that he had not been summoned sooner but Sarah said that her husband insisted there was no need for that, that he would soon recover.

At the inquest at the Gun Inn, death was said to be the result of strangulation of the intestines and recorded as being from natural causes. Sarah must have felt some sense of relief at this stage.

After all, she had poisoned her husband.

There was a brief interlude when she might have felt herself partially secure. She had been agitated about the inquest result. She had expressed her anxiety to some of her neighbours. But once that had produced a verdict of death from natural causes and once her husband had been buried she must have believed herself almost safe. But the doubts were too great, the whispers too loud. There was talk about poison being bought.

And, of course, young James Hickman was spoken about. He had been a regular visitor to the Frenchs and it had been noticed.

Then, during the fortnight after her husband's death, Sarah moved to a cottage on Popp's Farm, three quarters of a mile or so from her old home. Did she move so that she and Hickman would have more discreet opportunities to meet each other? Popp's and West Street Farm where Hickman lived and worked were very close together.

On 17 January, in the evening, Simon Peter Lower, schoolmaster and vestry member fulfilling the role of parish constable, called at Popp's Farm. He had come to escort Sarah to the Gun Inn. Another inquest had been convened.

'I suppose you have heard the rumours?' he asked her.

'You mean about my husband?'

Of course she had heard the rumours. Who had not?

There is no record of what passed at this evening inquest at the Gun Inn. Sarah was kept there overnight but allowed to return home the following day with matters unresolved.

Two days later, Superintendent Flanagan of East Sussex Police went to Popp's and escorted Sarah in a cart to the Six Bells at Chiddingly where the second inquest was resumed. Her husband's body had been exhumed. Dr Holman had carried out a post mortem examination and the body of William French now lay in the belfry of Chiddingly church.

This second inquest was once more adjourned but this time Sarah was taken into custody and lodged in Lewes gaol.

The whole of the stomach and intestines were sent for analysis to Professor Alfred Taylor at Guy's Hospital. The inquest was reconvened on

2 February when Professor Taylor presented his findings to the coroner and jury at the Six Bells in Chiddingly.

Professor Taylor estimated that up to eleven grains of arsenic had been administered. Three or four were enough to kill a man, he said. In his view French might have been given it in several small doses but he was confident that one large dose had been administered in the twenty four hours before death.

A variety of witnesses now appeared before the Coroner – doctors, neighbours, shopkeepers – all of them attesting to the fact that French had generally been a healthy man. Among the most powerful statements were those of William Funnell and Henry Hickman, father of James.

Funnell told the court:

'About Christmas he (French) told me that young Hickman was always at his house and he had spoken to his (Hickman's) father about it. He appeared to be uneasy in his mind, but did not say why he was so. He was a very quiet man and not much given to talking.'

Later, Henry Hickman told the court:

'I had a conversation with the deceased on the Sunday week before he died. I met him coming from chapel; he was alone; it was towards one o'clock. He overtook me and I said: "Well, Mr.French, how be you?"

He replied: "Not very well."

'I asked him who that was before us.

'He said: "It is my wife and your Jim" and he said "I don't very well like it."

'I said: "No more do I."

'He said then: "I wish you would tell him to keep away from my house."

'I asked if he ever saw any underhand dealings between my son and his wife.

'He said: "No."

'I said: "He tells me you asked him to come and read a book to the little boy who was ill."

He said: "I did."

'I asked him why he did not tell him to keep away if he did not like it. He said the reason why he did not tell him to do so was, if he spoke to his wife she would say he was jealous of her and he thought she would make away with herself.

'The following Sunday I saw the deceased going to chapel with his wife arm-in-arm. . .I told my son what Mr French had said, and he replied, if

Mr. French had told him he did not want him to come he would not have gone.

'I have frequently told him not to go there. He said French had asked him to go and read to his little boy who was ill.'

After this James Hickman admitted at the inquest that he and Mrs French sometimes kissed, that she sometimes sat on his knee, that they had talked of marriage, that he had been at the house on the night that French ate the onion pie. Hickman was also to say that he heard the sick man upstairs, retching and vomiting violently on the night he died.

It did not take the inquest jury long to return a verdict of wilful murder against Sarah French and she was committed for trial at the Sussex Spring Assizes.

❏ ❏ ❏ ❏ ❏ ❏

Sarah was seriously ill while awaiting trial. When she appeared before Mr Baron Parke at the Assizes at Lewes on 19 and 20 March, 1852, she presented a forlorn figure.

'The prisoner was paralysed and would require to be seated. She appeared greatly changed since her committal having lost all her colour.' She was never to recover her health.

There were two main strands to the case. The first concerned the poison, how and where it was purchased and by whom. The second related to Sarah's liaison with Hickman and whether he had played any part in the murder.

In the waiting period, on 19 February, Sarah had made an unexpected and dramatic statement about James Hickman. In this she said that he had confessed to her that on two occasions he had administered poison to her husband – once in the onion pie, once in his gruel.

Another time, when she was complaining about French being out late at night, she said that Hickman had told her he would give him something that would make him stay out later.

Sarah also claimed that Hickman had shown her a package of arsenic. He had threatened to leave her if she told anyone what he had said. These allegations were read to the court early in the proceedings.

In the two weeks before French's death, there was certainly arsenic in the cottage. The poor man had bought some to get rid of an infestation of mice. French had asked Sarah to hide the arsenic for fear their six year old son found it. When French had arrived home with the arsenic, James

Hickman was present, which some might have considered significant.

It was, however, Sarah's purchase of arsenic which concerned both the inquest and the Assize Court. Evidence was brought that she had purchased the poison on 5 January. Had the half ounce that French had brought home only a fortnight earlier been used up? Had some of it been in the Christmas Eve Onion Pie, that 'rarity' which he had so much looked forward to?

Two days before her husband's death, Sarah had walked to Horsebridge where Naomi Crowhurst, the vet's wife, reluctantly sold her two pennyworth of white arsenic. Learning that it was for mice, Mrs Crowhurst warned Sarah of its dangers, writing 'Poison' on the bottle.

Sarah denied at both inquest and trial ever having been in Crowhurst's shop. Other witnesses were called to say that they had seen Sarah on the Horsebridge road that day. She conceded that she had gone there to buy ribbons. Perhaps she had. But she was also the woman who had bought twopennyworth of arsenic from Mrs Crowhurst. There was strong evidence from both Mrs Crowhurst and the shop girl who recognised Sarah as their customer.

After Sarah's statement accusing him of the murder, James Hickman becomes a figure of even greater interest at the trial than he had been at the inquest.

He is described in *The Times* as having 'the appearance of a labouring man'. The *Sussex Express* says: 'He is about 18 years of age but scarcely looks as old as that.' Here then is this boyish figure, really a twenty year old, who in the eyes of those present might have been French's poisoner. Here was the man whose relationship with Sarah had worried not only French but his own father.

Hickman had first come to know the Frenchs well in the last year. At that time he had been courting Sarah's sister, Jane Piper, then aged about seventeen.

When Jane came to stay at the French's cottage, Hickman visited her there. Much was made at the trial about when this relationship foundered and that with Sarah started up. Possibly there was a period when Hickman was setting his cap at both ladies.

Perhaps it is reasonable to date the start of the affair between Sarah and Hickman from autumn 1851, making it a romance of a quite short duration. On both of his appearances, before the coroner and the judge, Hickman was at pains to imply that Sarah took all of the initiatives.

'She asked me if I liked her as well as I did her sister.

'I said "No" and she said, "Why not?"'

'I then said: "Because you are married."'

'She then asked me if I should like her if she was not married and I told her I liked her very well. This was about a month before Christmas.'

Hickman had taken to visiting the cottage two or three times a week, spending an hour or so there. Sometimes Sarah had turned up at West Street Farm asking him to visit. On occasions he seems to have gone out for a drink with French although it is apparent from the evidence of William Funnell and Henry Hickman that there must have been a cooling off in the friendship of the two men. Often Hickman read to little James French and this was one of the reasons given for the frequency of his visits.

From time to time when they were alone, Hickman told the court, Sarah would kiss him. At other times she would sit on his knee. Nevertheless, the young man was quick to say that he did not always respond.

He was, of course, anxious now to distance himself from Sarah who had tried to blame him for her husband's death. Asked if she ever 'made free with him' in her husband's absence, he replied that 'she never pulled me about improperly'.

Before William French's death, Hickman was given a ring by Sarah to keep in remembrance of her and this was produced in court. There was some conversation, too, about future marriage. What would he do, Sarah had asked him, if her husband died?

'I told her I did not know. I did not mind much about it,' Hickman told the court, carefully detaching himself.

He was being pursued as a prospective bridegroom immediately after French's death, he said. On the night of French's burial, Sarah was asking Hickman to marry her. They had better wait a twelvemonth, he had told her. It would look better.

On the night of the funeral, for the first time, she and Hickman shared a bed. This was the first occasion that sexual intercourse had occurred. What disturbed the court greatly, however, was to learn that on this night, when Hickman and Sarah came together as lovers for the first time, their bed was shared by Jane Piper and that little James French's bed was in the same room.

One explanation for the bed sharing on 11 January – and there was a bed in the kitchen in addition to that upstairs – may be that on this night of emotion, highly charged after the recent events, Sarah needed the comfort not just of James Hickman but also of her younger sister.

Sarah French, guilty of murder, anxious perhaps about rumours, feeling even now only partially safe after her husband's burial, was no doubt a confused woman, seeking solace from the two people she most certainly loved.

During the next few days, the lovers slept together on several occasions, first at the cottage in Gun Hill and later at Popp's Farm.

Mr Rodwell, defending Sarah, suggested to the jury that there was no proof of her having poisoned her husband. It could have been Hickman whom Sarah had accused in her statement before the trial began.

Rodwell argued that Hickman might have been after a share of a legacy of £500 which apparently was coming to Sarah. She had told Hickman that she would keep him, that he would never need to work again. Indeed it was a considerable sum although whether it existed, and whether Hickman believed in its existence, is not known.

It took the jury an hour and three quarters to reach a conclusion. Finally they returned a verdict of guilty although the foreman made the judge aware that some of the jurymen believed her to be more an accessory before the fact rather than the principal agent.

It was enough for the judge. Even if she had not put the poison in her husband's food, he declared that if she knew of someone else who was carrying out such a crime she was guilty of wilful murder.

She was sentenced to death.

Sarah French, 4ft 10ins in height, was described for the first time in *The Times* on the day the verdict was announced: 'The prisoner, although stated in the calendar to be only 27 years old, bears all the appearance of a woman of 40 and her countenance is one of the most repulsive character.'

But then perhaps *The Times* believed that criminals of the lower class ought to look repulsive, that their vices, their criminality, ought to be etched in their faces. As it is we have no reliable description of Sarah French save that she was a tiny woman. She was ill after being taken in custody and remained so for the few remaining days of her life.

As for James Hickman, the press emphasised his lack of emotion. He made no kind of response when he heard 'his wretched paramour's fate'.

Yet how should he react? Should he appear to approve of the sentence? Or distressed as though he too were guilty? Certainly by now he must have fallen out of love with Sarah in view of her having tried to implicate him.

How do twenty year old country boys know what expressions they ought to show in front of the full and fearsome majesty of the law?

Hickman's statements in court do sometimes conflict.

Did he or did he not agree to marry Sarah if her husband were to die?

Was he or was he not surprised at French's death?

Did he never suspect anything?

As far as he knew, he said, French had 'something bad the matter with him and the doctors could not do him any good'. Sarah had told him this and he had believed her. She had said to him that her husband 'was frequently taken very bad in his inside at night and that it would kill him'. It does seem that James Hickman never doubted her until perhaps after her arrest.

On the day before her execution, Sarah confessed to the prison chaplain that she alone had poisoned her husband, that Hickman had had no part in it and that she had implicated him solely with the idea of 'making matters lighter with herself'.

Sarah French hanged at Lewes Gaol on 10 April, 1852. A crowd of more than three thousand, some of them arriving from distant parts by train, crowded the town. The windows of all the houses facing the prison were filled with spectators.

They saw Sarah's frail figure carried to the scaffold, saw her supported there over the trapdoor, saw her struggles which lasted some minutes as she choked at the rope's end, saw her body finally taken down. The corpse was then placed in a lead coffin and buried within the outer walls of the prison.

James Hickman returned to West Street Farm. Later he married, had a family, lived in a cottage in Gun Hill and continued working as a farm labourer.

The Onion Pie Murder, as it is sometimes called, touched a whole close-knit world, stained some lives. Even the great world beyond heard of it, read about it. It was a cruel murder committed by a very ordinary woman who, until the last turbulent months of her life, had the reputation of being a loving wife, a caring mother and a good neighbour.

Was she simply an uneducated peasant woman caught up in a whirl of emotions beyond her control, a woman who in the space of a few months was cast in the role of a major character in a minor, sordid, rural tragedy? Was she no more than a sad, obsessed, misguided woman betrayed by her passions?

Was that how it was?

GLEANINGS 1851

4 January 1851

Emma Smith, 16, single woman, was charged with stealing on 6th September, at Uckfield, two Common Prayer books, two Hymn books, ten children's books, etc., the property of John Foster, her master – Four months' hard labour, except four weeks' solitary.

18 January 1851

Eliza Bonniface (Colgate Forest), a woman about 40 years of age, and as rough and wild as a forest colt, appeared to a summons for having, on Monday 6th inst., unlawfully and maliciously injured a calf, the property of Thomas Gent, by cutting it with a heath hook. Fine 5s. or one months' confinement.

Jonah Bonniface, son of the defendant in the previous case, and about 16 years of age, was committed to Petworth for one month, for setting a wire for the purpose of catching game.

1 February 1851

Robbery – A new system of robbery has recently sprung up in Brighton, which should put people on their guard. The thieves make use of newly finished uninhabited houses adjoining. On Friday evening last, the attic of 6 Upper Brunswick Place, the residence of Mr. Henry Smithers was entered by this means, the thieves having to pass over the tops of three or four houses to obtain access to the upper apartments of Mr. Smithers' house, from which they carried off a quantity of wearing apparel and a brooch.

15 February 1851

Alfred Witten, a little urchin, aged eleven years, was charged with stealing ducks eggs belonging to Mr. Breach. Poiney deposed that Mr. Breach, complaining that he had lost several eggs, he offered to watch, and on the morning of the 28th he saw the prisoner crawl through the hedge and take two from a nest: he laid them down and was just pulling his shoes off to go into the pond after another when Poiney pounced on him.

The boy was ordered to be taken to the lock up and once privately whipped by the police officer. The boy's father was in court and told he might be present when the punishment was inflicted.

12 April 1851

Stephen Doust, P.C. – I recollect the Rodmill Club night on the 20th May. The club is held at the Abergavenny Arms. About ten at night I was sent for to quell a disturbance between parties who had previously been quarrelling. I was thrown down on the floor, and one of the party, William Robinson, thrust his fingers in my throat. I had about ten men on top of me. The prisoner at the bar, when I was released, followed me out of the door, and I heard him say, 'A ring, a ring' and he pulled his clothes off. A party closed round, amongst whom was the prisoner. I was knocked down and I am quite sure the prisoner was one of the men who struck at me. My staff was taken from me but I am not aware whether or not I was struck with it. I was under the care of a surgeon for more than a week.'

17 May 1851

Mr. Holman deposed – I was returning home last evening, about a quarter before five o'clock, along the Eastbourne road, in my pony chaise, accompanied by my son Thomas who is aged 11 years. At a spot about three quarters of a mile before East Hoathly village, between two woods, I saw the prisoner come upon the road about 20 yards in front of me, from behind some bushes on the right hand side of the road. He came across a swampy piece of ground in the direction of my chaise with his right hand in his jacket pocket. I whipped the pony and drove faster. When I came on a level with him, he pulled a pistol from his pocket and presented it. He said, 'Stop, stop, your money or ——.'

I was riding rather fast and my pony being a spirited animal, I got out of hearing. I got the constable and several persons to go immediately in pursuit. I accompanied them and came up with the man in about an hour afterwards at Laughton Pound. Mr. Starnes (the constable) took the man into custody. He struggled with Starnes and got away and threw away a bundle. We then discovered that it contained a jacket, a pistol and some other articles.

18 October 1851

GEORGE GATTON, errand boy, 16, pleading guilty to stealing on the 8th October, at Brighton, one pocket-book containing five notes, the property of Robert Goulding. – *Two months hard labour except two weeks' solitary.*
MARY SKINNER (on bail) pleaded guilty to stealing on the 2 September, at Lamberhurst, three gallons of coals, the property of Jeffrey Playfoot. – *One week's solitary.*

9 August 1851

EMBEZZLEMENT – On Wednesday last Alfred Styles, an old man of 80, was charged before the Mayor with embezzling 7s., the money of his master, Charles Page. Mr Page sent him out for muffins, which the old man sold and made off with the money. On Tuesday last, Jessop apprehended him at Rye.

15 May 1852

A daring robbery was effected on Sunday morning last. Between nine and ten a fashionable dog cart, with three men, was observed near the entrance of the village of Henfield, when two of them alighted, and the other, with the trap, rode through the village as far as Wartley and back again, and put the horse up at the George Inn. The three men then perambulated the place and no doubt watched the Mrs. Harriott Harwood and her family to the church, they then unlocked the front door of her house, and deliberately walked in and broke several locks, taking and carrying away with them forty pounds worth of property in monies, silver plate and trinkets. Ordering the horse and trap they proceeded back to Brighton, and as it appears put the horse into the hands of Mr. Boss, livery stable keeper, whom they hired the same of. The family on sitting down to dinner found, to their surprise, the plate was missing.

The above extracts are from the *Sussex Agricultural Express*.

BIBLIOGRAPHY

Albion's Fatal Tree by D Hay, P Linebaugh and E P Thompson, Penguin 1975.

An Authentic and Faithful History of the Murder of Celia Holloway by John Holloway 1832.

Captain Swing by Hobsbawm and Rudd. Penguin 1973.

Crime and Society in England by Clive Emsley. Longman 1987.

Crime in Early Modern England by J A Sharpe. Longman 1983.

Forest Row – Historical Aspects and Recollections, Vol 2, Part 2, 1985.

History of Horsham by William Albery.

History of Sussex by Thomas W Horsfield 1835.

Life in Brighton by Clifford Musgrove, Hallewell 1981.

Popular Protest and Social Crime by Roger Wells. Southern History, Vol 13 1991.

Quarter Sessions Papers. East Sussex County Record Office.

Rogues and Vagabonds by Lionel Rose, Routledge 1988.

Royal Foliage by Molly Pears 1959.

The Trials of the Rev Robert Bingham by J M Richardson 1811.

The Victorian Underworld by Kellow Chesney. Temple Smith 1970.

Brighton Gazette
Brighton Guardian
Brighton Herald
Sussex Agricultural Express
Sussex Weekly Advertiser
The Times

Front cover: Public executions went on until 1868 and attracted crowds of onlookers. Souvenir prints, like this one of a double hanging, found a ready market.